BORN-AGAIN
VINTAGE

BORN-AGAIN VINTAGE

25 WAYS TO DECONSTRUCT, REINVENT + RECYCLE YOUR WARDROBE

+ + + BRIDGETT ARTISE + JEN KARETNICK + + +

POTTER
CRAFT

NEW YORK

Published in the United States by Potter Craft,
an imprint of the Crown Publishing Group, a division
of Random House, Inc., New York.
www.pottercraft.com

POTTER CRAFT and colophon is a registered trademark
of Random House, Inc.

Library of Congress Cataloging-in-Publication Data
is available upon request.

ISBN: 978-0-307-40527-2
Printed in China

Design by Amy Sly
Photographs by Heather Weston

10 9 8 7 6 5 4 3 2 1

First Edition

FOR MY CUSTOMERS FROM ALL OVER WHO
BELIEVE IN B. ARTISE.

PHOTOGRAPHER HEATHER WESTON

STYLIST KRISTEN PETLISKI

HAIR AND MAKE-UP JULIA JOSEPH

TABLE OF

ACKNOWLEDGMENTS 9
INTRODUCTION 10
WHERE TO BUY VINTAGE 14

CHAPTER 1 WINTER 18
BOOT PANTS 20
WINTER VEST 22
SWEATER MINI-DRESS 24
SWEATER SLIPDRESS 26
LEG WARMERS 28
KNIT CAP WITH VISOR 30

CHAPTER 2 SPRING 32
SWEATER CORSET 34
CAPELET 36
T-SHIRT BLOUSE 38
CROPPED JACKET 40
WIDE BELT 42

CHAPTER 3 SUMMER 44
T-SHIRT DRESS 46
STRAPLESS TOP 48
BIB-FRONT TANK TOP 50
DENIM BAG 52
SHORT SHORTS 54

CONTENTS

CHAPTER 4 FALL — 56

MINI-PONCHO — 58
HIGH-WAISTED SKIRT — 60
SWEATER HOODIE — 62
VINTAGE COMBO DRESS — 64
ARM WARMERS — 66

CHAPTER 5 PRETTY IN A BLINK — 68

STRAPLESS MINI-DRESS — 70
VINTAGE JUMPER — 72
REMIX DRESS — 74
HALTER DRESS — 76

BORN-AGAIN VINTAGE PATTERNS — 78

WINTER — 80
SPRING — 92
SUMMER — 101
FALL — 111
PRETTY IN A BLINK — 120

HELPFUL RESOURCES — 132
VINTAGE OUTFITTERS — 133
GLOSSARY — 143
INDEX — 144

ACKNOWLEDGMENTS

My children, TYLER-MARIE and L.J., are the driving force behind every good thing I have achieved, so I thank them for being great kids—even during not-so-great times.

I have friends that are straight from a fairytale: NITA YARBRO, ANGELA BAKER, LITA JOHNSON, and NANETTE BOGGAN. Your support and belief in me are truly appreciated.

PASCAL, thank you for helping me, sharing your time, and being patient with me when I asked for more than you could do.

DOMINI ORESKI, who lends her ear but never judges, thank you.

MELISSA LIM, my pattern editor, thank you for joining me late in the game and coming through to save the day.

Thank you to JEN KARETNICK, my right hand in this process who never once made me feel like a pain when I knew I was.

Many thanks to ROSY NGO, who stumbled across my clothing in SoHo and appreciated my talent enough to give me a chance.

A big thank you to my editor, COURTNEY CONROY, for putting up with my redundant questions without ever being bothered.

Tremendous thanks to AMY SLY for a gorgeous book design.

And, of course, countless thanks to the countless people and customers who inspire and encourage me: LISA SELLERS, JUDITH + FRANK LEWIS, BARBARA PETERS, SUSAN RAGBIR, JEANNE ANTOINE, HILDA BAKER, PAMELA MITCHELL, WAYNE FARQUHARSON, ALAN HORVATH, SIOBHAN BAILEY, DEBRA THOMPSON, CRYSTAL and SHELLY, RAOUL CALLEJA, MRS. C, and RUTH LEON, to name just a few.

INTRODUCTION

My clothing line, B. Artise Originals, is a product of my love for vintage duds but also my frustration with them. Period-dated, era-related clothing is great, but how many people can really pull it off? Whether the pieces aren't in good shape or their fit is less than ideal, vintage clothing can be challenging. Some designers try to fix that with reconstruction: reworking the older piece, fixing the places that are worn. There are also designers who incorporate new fabric, coordinating with the flow of the older piece.

Not me. At its simplest level, *Born-Again Vintage* is about turning antique and disused clothing into stylish togs by deconstructing it, choosing its best elements, and piecing those together with those of other garments. I'll completely rip out the seams of one basic vintage item and put it back together with a second, perhaps more contemporary piece to create an entirely different look. In this way, an old-fashioned ruffled shirt or a frumpy fifties housedress with terrific buttons—plus a tank top you can pick up at a wholesale store—can become a funky top; a poodle skirt and your so-last-year's knee-length cardigan sweater can be turned into anything from a

poncho to a structured tube top. My niche is bringing together the matchless quality of vintage with a dash of trendiness and edge to create a fashion-forward conversation piece.

What also sets my designs apart from the ho-hum, cookie-cutter styles you see everywhere is the juxtaposition of two fabrics that nobody else would dream of. I'm not bound by the standard rules of fashion (where stripes shouldn't go with polka dots or summer fabrics are never paired with heavier winter fabrics). My decision to explore fashion without boundaries gives me endless possibilities. When there are no rules, the only thing left is the freedom to create what feels right and looks good.

That's the essence of *Born-Again Vintage*.

But the reference to faith is no accident. The personal challenges I've conquered have given me new faith not only in life but in my own abilities. Prior to designing, I did very little that associated my passion for fashion with a career, and my path was somewhat foggy and unclear. However, through the pain of losing a loved one, my interest in clothing design came to the fore as a coping mechanism.

"Born-again" for me means being given a second chance at happiness. It is therefore no accident that I use old clothing in my designs. I want to give it second chances at life, too! Just because something may have lost its luster or is hanging in the back of your closet doesn't mean that you should give up on it.

So do as I do and don't limit yourself by thinking in predictable ways. Do you like the seventies-era zebra stripe dress in that consignment shop but can't see yourself rocking an animal print head to toe? Well, you're not going to be wearing it as is, so buy it! There are plenty of opportunities here for using that material in ways you may not have considered before. Love just a collar or a trim or even a belt? The ideas in *Born-Again Vintage* call for all sorts of scraps, from pockets to pant cuffs. In a way, these projects are like therapy. You'll be tackling them, at least vision-wise, one piece at a time. Then, as you get closer to finishing your new garment, it's both exciting and gratifying to see the culmination of your work and creativity.

The greatest part is that you don't have to spend a ton of money. Take a look in your closet and your dresser drawers. Pull out any old sweaters, skirts, and dresses you're not wearing anymore. Do they have some potential? If not, hit the thrift stores and sift through sweaters, keeping in mind that you don't necessarily have to find a perfect, unstained item or even the right size for a lot of these patterns. What matters is that you love the fabric or the details or the color. Swing by a wholesale store to buy inexpensive plain tank tops and T-shirts that you can use to refashion your vintage pieces. If you have too many for your own use, make gifts for all your friends. You'll be pleasantly surprised how economical your holiday season turns out to be.

The important thing to remember about *Born-Again Vintage* is to be unique. You can follow the patterns over and over again, but by changing the colors, the fabrics, and the accessories, each project will look absolutely fresh and completely different. So get out your scissors and start cutting. Soon your entire wardrobe will be reborn.

WHERE TO BUY VINTAGE

If you're not already a collector of vintage clothing, you might not know just where to start looking for pieces to get you going on your projects. Here are some tips everyone can use to score the hottest vintage finds.

Avoid trendy vintage boutiques. Since wearing period clothing became fashionable, these hip shops, most of which are located in high-rent areas, have been forced to raise their prices due to over-consumption by vintage scavengers. Not only that, the items they carry have usually been rehabbed—visible flaws fixed and stains sponged off—so their costs are also justified on the labor end. These are the pieces you want to wear as is, not cut up for the buttons, pockets, or that really neat lace collar.

Instead, go to the same sources as vintage boutique owners. They have to get their stock somewhere, right? You might as well do it just as cheaply. Here's how:

Visit estate sales. Sounds grand, we know, but "estate sale" is really just a fancier term for a garage sale. Except in this garage sale, everything—from every room in the house—has to go. Estate sales can range in style from auctions, where you bid on lots, to cash-and-carry whatever you fancy. Many times they are held because the owner of a home, or estate, has passed away, and the facilitator of the sale wants to turn belongings into cash.

Whatever the reason, you can usually assume that ridding closets full of decades-old clothing and accessories that once belonged to elderly women and men are part of the agenda. Antique and vintage dealers show up at these sites to buy in bulk, so at some heavily advertised sales you might expect competition. But at others, advertised only by fliers in your neighborhood or an advertisement in your local newspaper, you just might be one of the few who is interested.

Stop at garage sales. If you're less into organized hunting and more into spontaneous vintage-spotting, pull over for the random garage sale now and then. Even if you don't see a rack of clothing, folks often put out boxes of old sweaters and other clothing they've had in the attic for years. Lots of times, they have no real idea what's in there. You can often pick up a few items for pocket change—well worth the effort even if you're just going to unravel something and reuse the yarn.

If you're short on time, eBay is your best bet. The auctions on this site are the electronic answer to estate and garage sales, with the added advantage of your being able to sort by category. If you like surprises, don't hesitate to purchase lots of clothing from someone's grandmother's closet or jewelry chest for a mere ten dollars. Chances are you'll find a ton of fabric, plus at least one or two usable accessories—a fringe here, a pin there that can be converted to a closure—that will provide endless options for your *Born-Again Vintage* projects.

Don't underestimate the Salvation Army. Ditto for Goodwill or any secondhand store that benefits the underprivileged. Flipping through the racks and digging in the cartons in these warehouse-like operations can be time-consuming but also incredibly rewarding. You'd be surprised how much valuable vintage designer clothing is given away by people who don't know better (or who just want to get rid of it). These things aren't practical for the modern kid or mom who just wants to blend in at school or the workplace—they're looking for jeans and T-shirts, a business suit, or dress—but they're perfect for you! And they're darn cheap, too. Don't feel guilty, either. You're not taking clothing meant for somebody else; in fact, whatever you spend goes toward helping the less fortunate.

Finally, browse in antique shops. Most of these shops don't deal in large amounts of clothing—garments aren't a big draw in places that tend to specialize in furniture or china or glass—but every once in a while a closet's contents come with the deal if the buyer has purchased an entire bedroom lot, for example. So many shops do tend to have a rack of clothing, and these things are priced to move. If you don't see one? Ask. Sometimes a jacket with the most cunning little collar is stuck in a drawer in that lovely old dresser.

CHAPTER 1 WINTER

When it comes to keeping warm, there are some things that never go out of style—layering clothes, and bundling up, for example. I look forward to pulling out the coats and heavy sweaters and scarves every year when winter rolls around. It's also a great time to experiment with hats, scarves, and other cold-weather accessories. But while a typical pullover sweater or cardigan may never become outdated, the color or the houndstooth print on it will. In this chapter, we explore how to find a fashionable use for that plaid, ankle-length skirt you once adored, breathe new life into the leg warmer, and even address the cumbersome issue of stuffing your pants into your tall boots with ease. So scour your closet and vintage stores for heavy sweaters, wool coats, tweed skirts, and velvet blazers, and get ready to create some gems that will have you wishing winter was just a little bit longer.

BOOT PANTS

Trying to stuff your jeans into your boots is tiresome, and the result can be bunchy and uncomfortable—thus the inspiration behind this item. Add a colorful sweater sleeve to the bottom of your jeans to create the look of a leg warmer while eliminating the struggle of "boot-horning" your cuffs. At the very least, you'll save a few extra seconds in the morning getting dressed!

INSTRUCTIONS ON PAGE 81

+

WINTER VEST

You could not live through the seventies without seeing some style of vest. This vest, made out of an old velvet blazer, pays homage to that era. By keeping a small cap sleeve, you create two looks. Not only can it be worn as a vest, but the slight sleeve allows it to be worn as a jacket as well. The look shown here combines modern and retro for a piece that's wearable with just about anything. The black blazer provides a modern edge while the chunky plaid honors the style of the seventies. You can choose whatever combination of fabrics suits your taste, so get creative and experiment with a variety of colors and textures.

INSTRUCTIONS ON PAGE 82

SWEATER MINI-DRESS

The mini-dress has evolved quite a bit since Twiggy showed up on the 1960s fashion scene with her mod look and micro-hemlines. Then the look was billowy, shift-like, and often paired with white knee-high boots. The 1970s feminist movement inspired the longer hemlines of the midi- and maxi-skirt. Later, the eighties gave rise to almost skin-tight lycra minis that could barely pass for clothing, while the nineties saw the reinvention of the sixties mini-dress as a baby-doll look. Now the fashion world draws from every decade to give us a variety of mini-dresses that range from sleeveless tunics to Empress waist print chiffons. Here, my interpretation takes into account both the contemporary clothes you probably have in your own closet and the collectible ones you can easily find in a thrift shop. For instance, by adding a plaid insert with large buttons to a typical cowl-neck sweater, you create your very own version of the mini-dress.

INSTRUCTIONS ON PAGE **85**

SWEATER SLIPDRESS

This design was inspired by the delicate drape of the slips dutifully worn by women in the 1950s. While the same silhouette is often borrowed for summer sundresses, I've used it here with cashmere and wool tweed to add a twist to the typical and an edge to the ordinary. This is a perfect example of how taking something traditional and adding color and texture makes it modern and unique.

INSTRUCTIONS ON PAGE 87

 +

LEG WARMERS

Who can see a pair of leg warmers without picturing *Flashdance*? Though they have made several comebacks over the years, leg warmers haven't changed much in shape. This is an accessory that was definitely in need of a makeover! Using sweater sleeves gives you more flexibility with color and fabric, as well as the option to coordinate with your outfit. Be sure to pick sweater sleeves with sturdy ribbing at the cuffs so that the leg warmers stay up. Adding the sock to it gives you choices on how you can wear it—in the shoe, gathered at the ankle, or fitted at the knee. You decide.

INSTRUCTIONS ON PAGE 89

KNIT CAP WITH VISOR

Even accessories can use a makeover every now and then. Instead of letting that once trendy trucker hat that's so passé or the gold lamé hat from your skating days (still a favorite, though you wouldn't be caught dead in it now) go to waste, revive your headwear by combining it with a knit cap. Your dated hat becomes a fashion statement that also just happens to be one-of-a-kind—your kind.

INSTRUCTIONS ON PAGE 91

CHAPTER 2 SPRING

As soon as the snow is cleared from the streets and the first truly warm day of the year hits, excitement fills the air. The hottest new trends from the runways make their debuts on the street. Thoughts of coatless nights, spring prints, and light, flowy fabrics make us almost giddy with ideas for your spring wardrobe. But while some spring classics continue to endure year after year, you might notice that a fashion magazine or two have placed designs that you thought would be around forever on the "Not Hot" or "Out" list. What to do with your favorite blouse that's suddenly been declared a fashion disaster? Try remixing it with something vintage for an extra-special tune up. Keep the elements you like most, and your remade blouse will not only be on everyone's "Hot" list, it'll be on everyone's "Most Wanted" memo as well. Delve deep into this chapter to find ways to create corsets from your too-small or accidentally shrunken sweaters. Or find out how to fashionably crop your jackets, or remake an old skirt into a chic capelet. After all, early spring nights might still be a little chilly.

SWEATER CORSET

Back in the 1800s, the corset was worn under your clothes to give a sleek, smooth silhouette. But now, thanks to Madonna, this garment works just as well as outerwear. There have been a slew of variations on the traditional corset since its introduction, but few have seemed dialed-down enough for every day, and most have felt just as restricting as those worn two centuries ago. Using a sweater allows you to suit your taste—neutrals create a subtly romantic look, while colorful or sequined sweaters make a bold and playful statement. Introducing the "today" corset, constructed from comfortable knitwear and ready to go from day to night.

INSTRUCTIONS ON PAGE 93

CAPELET

This open-neck style was introduced in the 1950s. The women's clothing designer Alberto Fabiani used it for the top of his coat in 1959. The classic construction, coupled with a heady splash of color, makes this capelet brilliantly contemporary.

INSTRUCTIONS ON PAGE **95**

T-SHIRT BLOUSE

Polyester and big collars scream vintage—and the seventies. But these types of period blouse prints, while fabulous, can be uncomfortably warm during the months of spring, not to mention the fact that they're a little too *Saturday Night Fever* for everyday wear. Keep only the best parts of these fabulously funky pieces—the collar and the print—to mesh the unique style of vintage with the comfort of a cotton T-shirt. Not only is this piece great worn casually with jeans, but tuck it into a pencil skirt and you are off to work.

INSTRUCTIONS ON PAGE **97**

 +

CROPPED JACKET

Who would have thought that the 1930s bolero jacket with shoulder pads would become one of the most popular jacket styles to date? We might have stopped calling them boleros and lost the shoulder pads, but the shape will always endure. Using a brocade coat keeps it vintage, while adding a fancy trim to the bottom makes it unique and trendy. Finally, turning a standard sleeve into a bell sleeve makes it simply fabulous.

INSTRUCTIONS ON PAGE 98

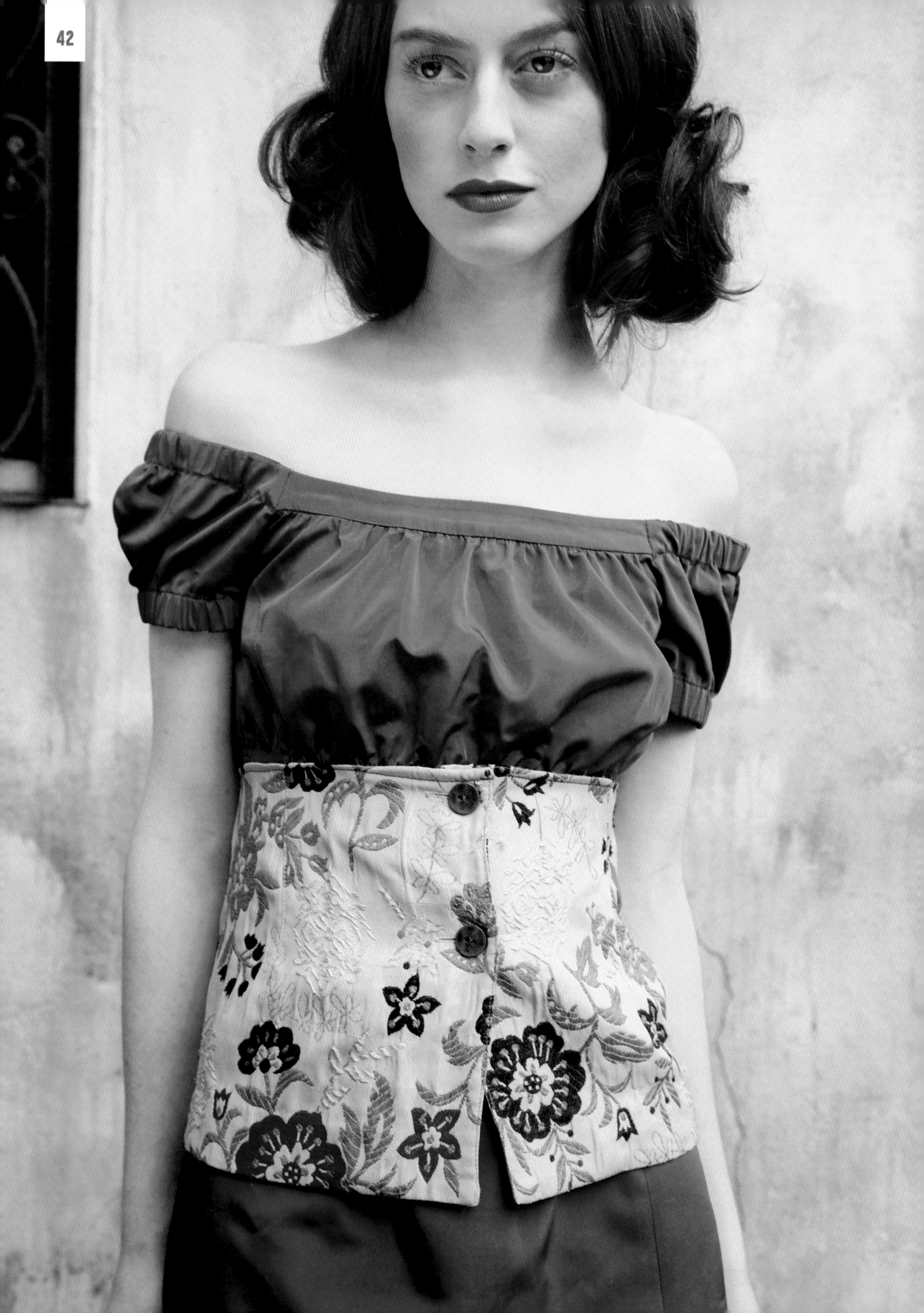

WIDE BELT

Belts have always been a go-to accessory. This one is more of a cross between a corset and a belt, giving you all the advantages of both—the hourglass waist plus a funky element to jazz up a plain dress. Use anything from an oversized blazer to an old, fitted dress to get this tailored look.

INSTRUCTIONS ON PAGE **100**

CHAPTER 3 SUMMER

Longer days, time in the sun, and lots of bare skin—summertime can be challenging to the style maven. But just because spaghetti straps and cutoff shorts are the order of the day doesn't mean you have to give up on your own inimitable fashion sense to dress like everybody else. Sure, tank tops, dresses, and jeans of all lengths make for no-brainer summer fashion. But with the ideas in this chapter for different silhouettes, distinctive embellishments, and the manipulation of fabrics not typically seen in summer months, you'll be creating head-turning pieces that make you feel like you're on the catwalk in no time.

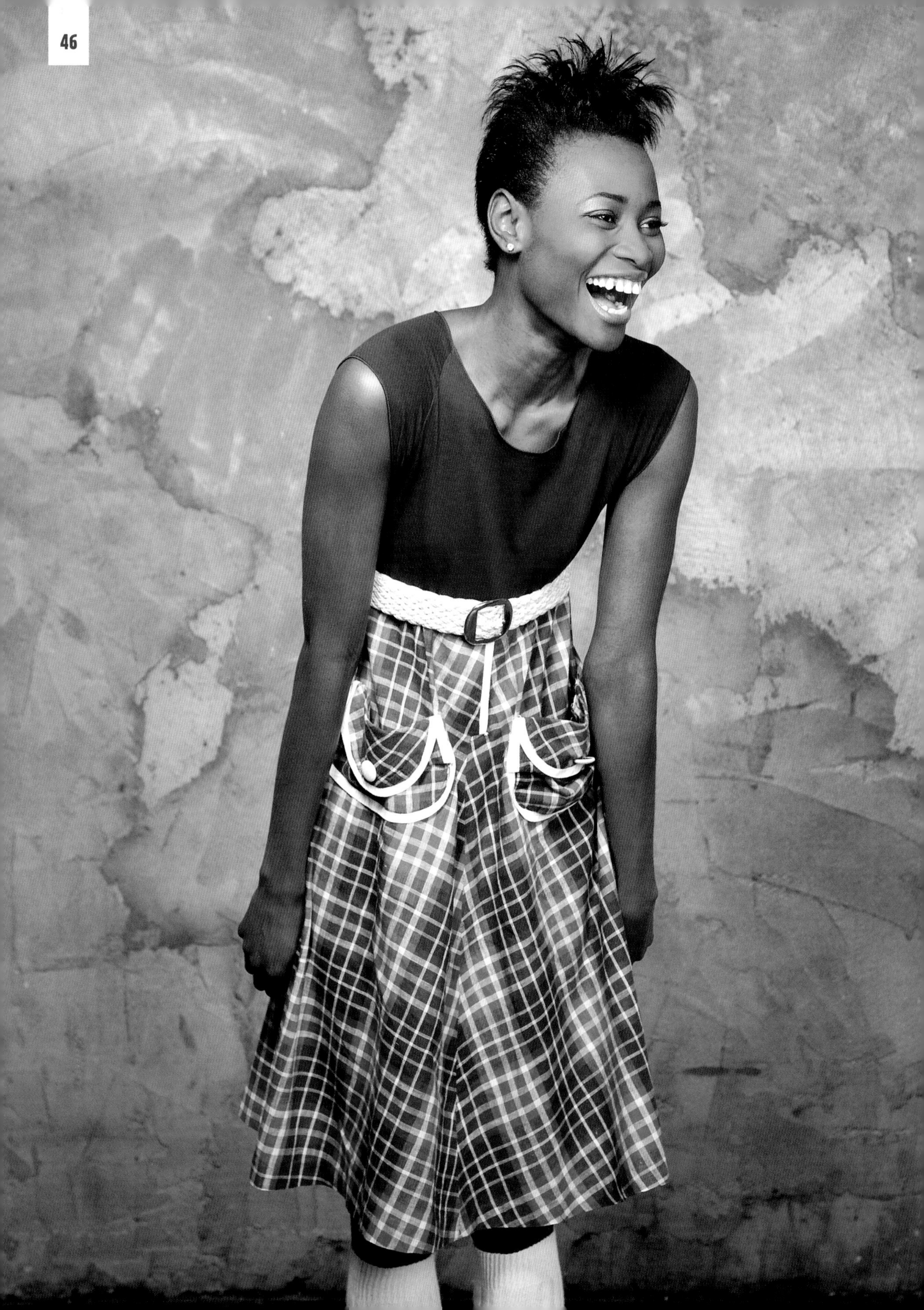

T-SHIRT DRESS

This is a great project for a housedress from the '40s or '50s. Take, for example, this 1947 button-through daywear dress with patch pockets that I found in C. Madeleine's, a terrific vintage consignment store in Miami. The allover plaid print, large pockets, and button-down style are about as dated as you can get. You might feel a little frumpy wearing it as is. But by incorporating a touch of modern edge with a T-shirt and a babydoll silhouette, you can turn this ho-hum housedress into a funky conversation piece.

INSTRUCTIONS ON PAGE 102

STRAPLESS TOP

At first, transforming a skirt into a top may be tough to imagine. But if you think about it, the elastic waistband and billowy folds of a vintage A-line skirt provide the perfect basis for a hot summer top. Throw in a funky vintage fabric and coordinating silk scarf to tie the look together, and you've got a quick and easy piece to wear day or night.

INSTRUCTIONS ON PAGE 103

BIB-FRONT TANK TOP

Using the same idea as the T-Shirt Blouse (page 39), this bib-style top uses less of the blouse and more of the tank top. This is a great alternative when you have a blouse that is stained or damaged, or if the collar is all that you like and want to take from the blouse. Many vintage blouses have great collars, so this design is perfect for them.

INSTRUCTIONS ON PAGE **104**

DENIM BAG

Just when you thought the denim tote was over and couldn't possibly be revived, here's a new twist on an old classic. The uses for and the variations of a denim bag are endless, especially when you make it with vintage jeans. Add a period belt as a strap, and you have just taken the typical denim bag to a whole new level.

INSTRUCTIONS ON PAGE **107**

SHORT SHORTS

The ever-evolving lengths of shorts can leave your head spinning. One year they are Bermudas; the next, Daisy Dukes. Both are from times past and represent different eras. But the latter is the one that seems to repeat over and over. Using a short-short pattern with any nostalgic print fabric or vintage piece adds a fresh twist and allows you to put your legs on full display.

INSTRUCTIONS ON PAGE **109**

CHAPTER 4 FALL

Autumn represents change. The leaves turn color, the weather starts to cool down, and the landscape changes from lush greens to deep hues like red, orange, and yellow. Still, it is a season that sparks new ideas. Perhaps it is because, while winter has accessories and summer has dresses, fall is known for colors—plum, burnt orange, khaki, and olive—that suggest fire and darkness, harvest, and rest. Or maybe it's because this time of year, clothing from the rest of the seasons can be mixed and matched. You can pull off wearing shorts with leggings, a tank top under a blazer, a scarf tucked into the neck of a blouse, or any other combination. So now, thanks to this chapter, the sweater whose spectacular color cannot be matched but that has stretched out beyond wearability finally gets to live another day, and the two dresses that you love equally (but that don't love you back like they did when you were a teenager) become one. And those nostalgic plaid minis you've been holding on to? Well, they finally see the golden light of a lovely fall day.

MINI-PONCHO

The poncho originated in Chile in the early 1700s, and it has been evolving ever since. Every now and again it disappears, then makes a comeback on the runways and in department stores. Here the mini-poncho takes another step into the future. By remaking a vintage sweater into this charming version of the poncho, you can add a chic and modern update to the classic design.

INSTRUCTIONS ON PAGE **112**

HIGH-WAISTED SKIRT

What was called the wide waistband in the forties is now the high waist. Adding the ribbed section of one garment to the top of a dress re-creates the high-waisted look in an entirely new and innovative way. Throw in some buttons for a nautical touch, and you have pulled together two different looks from two different eras to create one incredible fashion statement.

INSTRUCTIONS ON PAGE **113**

SWEATER HOODIE

This handknit sweater with its offbeat batwing sleeves gets a makeover with the addition of a hood and fun floral-print terry-cloth accents. The hood and accents are removed in one piece and sewn into the sweater for an innovative look that comes together in no time. At first glance, the two items might seem like very different pieces, but they blend like yin and yang.

INSTRUCTIONS ON PAGE 115

VINTAGE COMBO DRESS

One dress is vintage 1940s and the other is vintage 1950s. Putting the two together using a two-tone style in which the top of the outfit tells one story and the bottom tells another creates an eclectic mix of vintage that is classic and new at the same time. Cutting any fabulous vintage dress is a risk, but the end result here shows that it is worth the gamble.

 INSTRUCTIONS ON PAGE **116**

ARM WARMERS

What happens when you mix long opera gloves circa 1915 and leg warmers from the 1980s? A new fashion accessory is born. Wear them under your coat or with a sleeveless top for a funky look that will also keep you warm.

INSTRUCTIONS ON PAGE **119**

CHAPTER 5 PRETTY IN A BLINK

Not everyone has a fairy godmother like Cinderella did to turn her rags into a beautiful gown. But just like Molly Ringwald's character did in *Pretty in Pink,* most of us have an old party dress we would give anything to magically transform. Some gowns you really can just wave a wand over: Add a fun belt, select a different style of shoe, and you've got a whole new look. But others need more finessing. For instance, shortening and changing the neckline makes a scary eighties dress a downright fashion miracle. Adding fabric to the skirt of your over-the-top vintage A-line dress and creating a dramatic backless look makes it both fuller and sleeker. Sometimes all you need is a good old-fashioned sewing needle—and some *Born-Again Vintage* vision—to crank it up a notch.

STRAPLESS MINI-DRESS

How many times have you been told "You'll wear it again" about a bridesmaid's dress? Quite a few, right? It may seem far-fetched, but these old frocks are great resources for reuseable fabric. Though the color and fabric of the dress used for this project is to die for, the silhouette reminds us of the prom fashions worn in John Hughes movies. Work some magic by turning a shapeless would-be cast-off into a funky empire-waist mini.

INSTRUCTIONS ON PAGE **121**

VINTAGE JUMPER

I'm sure your first question when you look at this "before" photo is "Why change this really pretty, totally intact dress?" Simple—because it represents the one that sits and sits and sits in the back of your closet, unworn since your junior prom. You think of giving the dress to Goodwill but hold on to it yet another year. Time to release it from its prison and give it a new lease on life! By putting pockets in this fun and flirty dress, you not only give it a unique update and a second chance, you'll give it the opportunity to come back with a vengeance.

INSTRUCTIONS ON PAGE 124

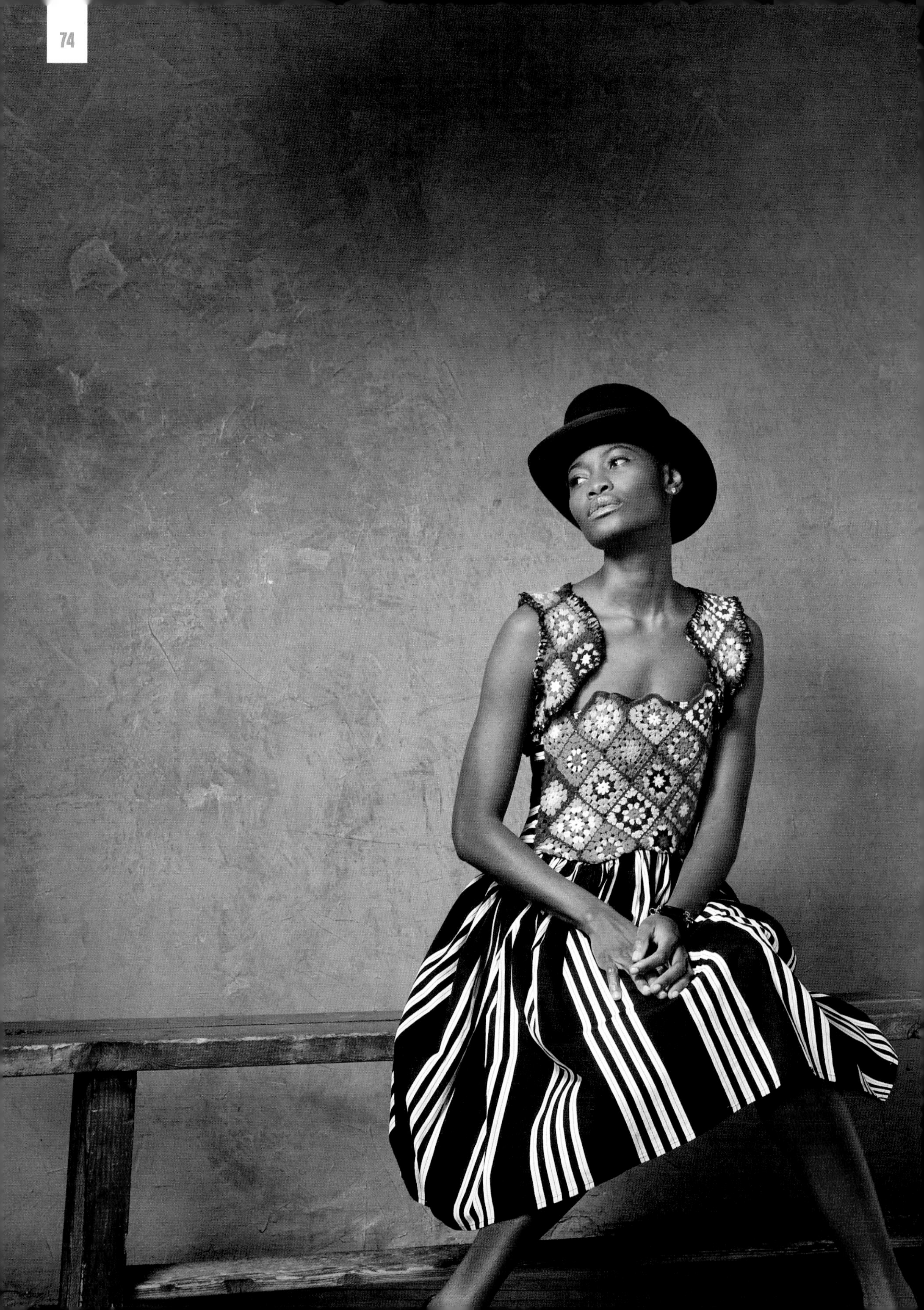

REMIX DRESS

With the other dresses in this chapter, our objective was to update them. With this dress, we wanted to add some vintage flair. We started with a standard striped summer dress, and just by adding crocheted patchwork fabric to it and a matching cropped bolero, it's revamped. Mixing the textures with a splash of color makes it something truly spectacular. Use your own design sense to come up with some fabulous combinations. Add a pair of hot vintage pumps and you are the center of attention.

INSTRUCTIONS ON PAGE 126

HALTER DRESS

Sometimes the silhouette, fabric, and color of a dress all combine for an overpowering effect—especially with the trends of yesteryear. Rather than pass up vintage gems like the one shown here, tone it down for an updated look. Here, we changed the silhouette by adding new fabric for a fuller skirt and removing some of the old fabric to create a sexy, backless look. Though it still says vintage, it is now wearable for a night out and no longer relegated to the annual costume party!

INSTRUCTIONS ON PAGE 130

PATTERNS

It'd be nice to think that all you have to do to magically turn your old clothes into new ones is to raid your closet and hit up a few vintage shops. However, a little work is required!

Fortunately, even for those who are "sewing machine illiterate," it's quite easy to accomplish a lot, which you'll see as you take a look at the patterns. They range from super-simple to sort-of complicated. At any skill level, you have at least a double handful of projects from which to choose.

The real beauty of this book is that there are no such things as mistakes; basically, this is a guide on how to free your imagination, so you should never feel overwhelmed by not getting something "right." One person's oopsie is another's pièce de résistance.

Another fabulous thing is that these projects will never become outdated. You can use different odds and ends each time to revamp your look. Plus, any and all leftovers—the tiniest scrap—can be reused for something else. Pretty soon, the ideas and instructions will become so ingrained you won't even need to glance back at the pages. That's when you'll truly know that you, too, have become *Born-Again Vintage*!

PATTERNS

CHAPTER 1
WINTER

BOOT PANTS

FITTED PAIR OF JEANS OR **PANTS + SWEATER WITH RIBBED CUFFS +**
RULER + TAILOR'S CHALK OR FABRIC PEN + SCISSORS + STRAIGHT PINS +
COORDINATING THREAD + SEWING MACHINE

PHOTO ON PAGE **20**

INSTRUCTIONS

1. Lay the jeans flat on the work surface with the front facing up. Measure and mark 10" (25.5cm) from the bottom of each pant leg. (If you're taller or shorter than average, you may want to adjust this measurement.) Cut off these bottom sections.

2. Lay the sweater flat on the work surface with the front facing up. Cut the sleeves off straight across from the underarms to the shoulders.

3. Turn the sweater sleeves inside out. Slide the sleeves over the bottom of each pant leg, so that the right sides are together and the cut edge of each sleeve lines up with the cut edge of the jeans. Match the seam of each sleeve with the inseams of the jeans. Pin into place.

4. Using a ¼" (6mm) seam allowance, machine-stitch the sleeves to the jeans. Finish the raw edges with a zigzag stitch or a serger. Remove the pins.

5. Fold the sleeves down and lightly press the new seams with an iron, if necessary.

TIP FOR A DIFFERENT LOOK, USE WIDE-LEG JEANS OR PANTS AND SEW IN GATHERS FOR MORE FULLNESS.

VINTAGE TWIST SCRUNCH THE SWEATER SLEEVES AT THE TOPS OF THE BOOTS TO CREATE THE LOOK OF LEGWARMERS.

PHOTO ON PAGE **23**

WINTER VEST

VINTAGE BLAZER + RULER + TAILOR'S CHALK OR FABRIC PEN + SCISSORS + STRAIGHT PINS + COORDINATING THREAD + SEWING MACHINE + **PRINT SKIRT** + 4 BUTTONS + NEEDLE

INSTRUCTIONS

1. Lay the blazer flat on the work surface with the front facing up. Measure and mark the sleeves 2" (5cm) from the shoulder seam. Cut off the sleeves and save them for another project.

2. Fold in the edges of the vest sleeves ½" (13mm) to create a finished hem. Pin into place. Sew close to the raw edge.

3. Lay the skirt flat on the work surface. Measure and mark a line around the skirt 2" (5cm) from the bottom edge. Cut off this strip of the skirt.

4. Cut two 7" (18cm)-long pieces from the strip and set aside the remaining piece, which will be used later. Because these sections were from the bottom edge of the skirt, one long side should already be hemmed. Finish the two shorter sides of one piece by folding them in ¼" (6mm) and pin into place. Machine-stitch close to the raw edges, no more than ¼" (6mm) from the edge. Repeat for the second strip.

VINTAGE TWIST IF YOU ARE USING A BLAZER WITH A PRINTED FABRIC, USE A SOLID SKIRT—OR GET FUNKY AND MATCH POLKA DOTS WITH STRIPES.

5. For each of the newly hemmed pieces, fold in the top raw edge ½" (13mm), so the fold is on the wrong side. Press. Place on the top hem of the vest pockets or as desired and pin to create pocket flaps. Sew the flaps to the pocket close to the folded edge, no more than ¼" (6mm) from edge.

6. Hand-sew the buttons onto each flap, one on each end of the pocket flaps.

7. To make the trim for the lapel, first measure the length of the lapel. Using the remaining strip of skirt fabric, cut a section that is equal to that length. Cut that piece in half lengthwise. On one long side, fold over a ½" (13mm) seam allowance and press. Then, with the right sides together, match the other long side edge to the lapel. Pin into place. Sew close to the edge, no more than ⅛" (6mm) from the edge.

8. Fold the fabric over and then under the lapel and press. Slip stitch the folded edge to the underside of the lapel.

TIP LESS IS MORE. DON'T FEEL LIKE YOU HAVE TO USE EVERY BIT OF THE SKIRT FABRIC. SAVE IT FOR ANOTHER PROJECT.

SIZING IT ALL UP

At some point during the last couple of decades you've probably heard the terms "VANITY SIZING" or "SIZE INFLATION." These phrases were coined in the late eighties and early nineties, when Hollywood and society women with physical features they considered embarrassing—big feet, for example—requested their shoes stamped with faux sizes.

Today the ready-to-wear industry happily caters to our egos and insecurities by plopping misleading labels on clothes TO MAKE US FEEL GOOD. And the better we feel, the more we buy. This strategy works particularly well with the more expensive stuff. So in general, while Americans are getting bigger, our designer duds are getting "smaller."

This phenomenon explains why ten years ago you were a size 10, and now, at relatively the same weight and height and perhaps after a kid or two, you're a 6. AT THAT SIZE, THOSE $300 JEANS ARE WORTH IT, RIGHT?

That might flatter you in a contemporary department store, but in a vintage boutique, it can frustrate you. Period clothes were cut to accommodate women who wore stricter undergarments than we do now. BODICES AND WAISTS CAN BE EXTREMELY NARROW because girls wore CORSETS, GIRDLES, AND OTHER TYPES OF BODY SHAPERS regularly, depending on the eras in which they lived. Don't think for one minute that the sizes of vintage clothes are going to correspond to either your current size or even the "size" you were ten years ago.

Think of it this way: You might have heard that MARILYN MONROE WAS A SIZE 12. Technically, that's an 8 in today's terminology. But take into account that nipped-in waist and fitted bodice, and you could probably comfortably wear one of her dresses only if you're smaller than a 6! And just to make matters more confusing, SOME VINTAGE SHOPS CARRY GOODS WITH EUROPEAN SIZING ON THE LABELS. Here, you need to know that a 42 is equivalent to a North American 12—but that's yesterday's 12, which is today's nonvintage 8 (and if it's a vintage piece, you better hope you're a hipless 4). So basically the clothes from ITALIAN, FRENCH, AND SPANISH DESIGNERS will be tighter than you might expect, if you judge by current standards.

In fact, that's a good guideline to apply to vintage shopping in general: ASSUME EVERYTHING IS TINIER THAN YOU THINK IT IS. Try on as much as possible, especially if you're in a boutique and shelling out big bucks for a preserved beauty of a dress; if you're in a thrift shop and dropping only a few dollars, IT'S WORTH TAKING A CHANCE, especially if you find something with great design details, but still try to guess on the large side. And don't let the sizes play head games with you. The only vanity you need here is the pride you can take in the finished piece.

SWEATER MINI-DRESS

TURTLENECK OR **COWL-NECK SWEATER** + TAILOR'S CHALK OR FABRIC PEN + SCISSORS + COORDINATING THREAD + SEWING MACHINE + **SKIRT** + STRAIGHT PINS + RULER + 6 SMALL TO MEDIUM COORDINATING BUTTONS OR 4 LARGE BUTTONS + SEWING NEEDLE

PHOTO ON PAGE **24**

INSTRUCTIONS

1. Try the sweater on, determine where the waist is, and mark with the tailor's chalk or fabric pen.

2. Lay the sweater flat, and cut straight across where it is marked. Set these two pieces aside.

3. Remove the sleeves by cutting them out at the seam. If the cut isn't even, sew a narrow zigzag stitch along the edges for a clean look.

4. Lay the skirt flat on the work surface and cut off the waistband. Avoid cutting the zipper. Next, determine how long you want the center section of the tunic to be—the one shown is approximately 10" (25.5cm) long. Measure the length and mark with the tailor's chalk or fabric pen.

5. Cut the skirt where it is marked.

TIP DON'T CUT THE SWEATER HIGHER THAN NATURAL WAIST LEVEL. SYMMETRY IS EVERYTHING WITH THIS LOOK.

VINTAGE TWIST IF THE SWEATER HAS SLEEVES, CUT THEM OFF AND USE THEM FOR LEG WARMERS (PAGE 89) OR ARM WARMERS (PAGE 119).

6. With the right sides together, line up the unfinished edges of the top of the skirt section with the bottom edge of the top sweater section. Pin into place.

7. Machine-stitch the pieces together using a $\frac{1}{4}$" (6mm) seam allowance.

8. With the right sides together, line up the unfinished edges of the bottom skirt section with the top edge of the bottom sweater section. Pin into place.

9. Sew the pieces together using a $\frac{1}{4}$" (6mm) seam allowance.

10. Finish the seams with a zigzag stitch or serger.

11. Press the seams lightly with an iron.

12. Using the tailor's chalk or fabric pen, mark the button placements on the center of the skirt panel so they are evenly centered and parallel to each other.

13. Hand-sew the buttons on.

SWEATER SLIPDRESS

RULER OR MEASURING TAPE + **SWEATER** + SCISSORS + COORDINATING THREAD + SEWING MACHINE + SEWING NEEDLE (OPTIONAL) + TAILOR'S CHALK OR FABRIC PEN + STRAIGHT PINS + **SKIRT**

PHOTO ON PAGE **27**

INSTRUCTIONS

1. Measure the distance from your shoulder to the beginning of your waist.

2. Cut the length of the sweater to match that measurement, adding 1" (2.5cm) for the seam allowance.

3. Cut the sleeves to the desired length. I recommend short or sleeveless.

4. To create the sleeve hem, fold the unfinished sleeve edge ¼" (6mm) to the wrong side once and then another ¼" (6mm) to hide the raw edge. Topstitch close to the finished edge, no more than ¼" (6mm) from the edge. You can also hand-sew the hem for a more polished look.

5. Fold the sweater in half lengthwise, lining up the shoulder seams, and pin into place.

VINTAGE TWIST USE THE EXCESS WAISTBAND TO MAKE PIPING FOR THE ARMHOLES AND A FUNKY COLLAR.

TIP ADD A WIDE VINTAGE BELT TO MAKE THIS DRESS EVEN HOTTER!

6. Mark and cut the desired neck shape. You can make a V-neck, as shown, or try a scoop neck, keyhole, or any style that will create the look you want. Fold the unfinished neck edge ¼" (6mm) to the wrong side and topstitch close to the raw edge, no more than ¼" (6mm) from the edge. Set the sweater aside.

7. Cut off the waistband of the skirt at the seam. Avoid cutting the zipper.

8. Measure and make a 2" (5cm)-wide mark at the bottom center back of the sweater.

9. With the right sides together, line up the unfinished edges of the sweater and the skirt and pin into place. Machine-stitch the two sections together, making sure the zipper is aligned in the center of the 2" (5cm) space at center back. DO NOT sew this 2" (5cm) opening closed. This opening will allow you to close the zipper on the skirt.

10. Finish the raw edges with a zigzag stitch or serger.

LEG WARMERS

SWEATER SLEEVES WITH RIBBING AT THE CUFF (LOOK FOR SWEATERS WITH FULLER SLEEVES) + SCISSORS + **SOCKS** (TUBE OR TROUSER) + STRAIGHT PINS + COORDINATING THREAD + SEWING MACHINE

PHOTO ON PAGE **28**

INSTRUCTIONS

1. Place the sleeves on top of each other, matching the cuff ends and seams. Cut the tops of the sleeves straight across (parallel to the cuffs) to create even edges and ensure both are equal in length.

2. Lay the socks flat on top of each other. Measure and cut 4" (10cm) from the top. Do not cut less than 4" (10cm).

3. Turn the socks inside out. Slide the sleeves over the socks, so that the right sides are together and the unfinished edges match. Stretch the socks to match the size of the sleeves. Pin into place.

4. Using a ¼" (6mm) seam allowance, machine-stitch the socks to the sleeves. Remove the pins. Finish the raw edges with a zigzag stitch or serger.

5. (Optional) With an extra pair of socks, repeat the instructions on the other side of the sleeve for a more secure fit.

TIP USE THE SWEATER SLEEVES FROM SWEATER TUNIC (PAGE 85) OR SWEATER SLIP DRESS (PAGE 87), OR CUT OFF THE SLEEVES FROM ANOTHER SWEATER.

VINTAGE TWIST TUBE SOCKS WORK BEST FOR A CASUAL, EVERYDAY LOOK. TRY MORE DECORATIVE TIGHT-KNIT SOCKS FOR A FUN WAY TO DRESS UP AN EVENING LOOK.

BEADS, BUTTONS, AND OTHER NOTIONS

Though they may sound inconsequential, notions are big business. From 1920S RED GABLONZ CZECH GLASS DRESS CLIPS to 1930S LEAF-GREEN ENGLISH CASEIN (BAKELITE) BUCKLES, ornaments for clothing are items that collectors fight over, and they can be quite pricey if unscrupulous dealers sense that they have an advantage over you. There are even clubs devoted to them that have bylaws—THE NATIONAL BUTTON SOCIETY, for instance, mandates that all buttons made after 1918 are modern, not antique.

YOU DON'T HAVE TO BE THAT SERIOUS-MINDED FOR BORN-AGAIN PROJECTS. One of the cool things about buying vintage wear is harvesting the knickknacks from the garments: jeweled buttons, embroidered or sequined patches, bugle- or seed-beaded appliqués, and fancy toggle closures, to name just a few. Transferring any of these embellishments to another piece of clothing—or even a shoe or purse—GIVES IT A ONE-MINUTE MAKEOVER. The ideas are limited only by your imagination.

Unless you're looking for something really specific—say, French Art Deco sequins on their original strands that you want to sew on individually—EYE YOUR VINTAGE PIECES AS THREE-FOR-ONE SPECIALS. You might be buying a sweater for its shell to make the Sweater Corset (page 93), but don't throw away that seed pearl collar or those Satsuma buttons. They're valuable bits that'll come in handy for other projects.

To save even more money, THINK OF YOUR VINTAGE SHOPPING LIKE A TREASURE HUNT. Look for details such as velvet or lace trim, yokes, cuffs, fichus, and jabots on garments that are stained and torn and in the bargain bin. AND BE SURE TO CHECK OUT THE DUDS THAT OTHERS OVERLOOK because they have little use for them: antique children's clothing that no twenty-first-century kids in their right Gap-oriented minds would wear; plus-size lingerie; patterned, beribboned aprons; stained gloves that button up the sides with pearls. THESE ARE THE REAL JEWELS.

KNIT CAP WITH VISOR

COORDINATING KNIT CAP + OLD BASEBALL HAT + STRAIGHT PINS + SCISSORS + SIZE 110/18 SEWING MACHINE NEEDLE; COORDINATING THREAD OR CHENILLE OR TAPESTRY NEEDLE; 8MM EMBROIDERY FLOSS

PHOTO ON PAGE **31**

INSTRUCTIONS

1. Place the knit cap on top of the baseball hat, making sure the edges of both hats line up perfectly. Cut and remove the crown of the baseball hat, leaving only the bottom sweatband.

2. Pin the sweatband inside the bottom edge of the knit cap.

3. Using a sewing machine, change the needle to a size 110/18 for heavy fabrics. Machine-stitch the knit cap to the sweatband.

   OR

   Using the tapestry needle, embroidery floss, and a running stitch, sew the pieces together.

TIP BE SURE TO REMOVE ANY CARDBOARD PIECES IN THE HAT BEFORE SEWING.

VINTAGE TWIST EMBELLISH YOUR HAT WITH A VINTAGE BROOCH OR BUTTONS AS SHOWN, OR HAND-STITCH YOUR OWN DESIGN.

PATTERNS
CHAPTER 2
SPRING

SWEATER CORSET

SWEATER + SAFETY PIN + TAILOR'S CHALK OR FABRIC PEN + STRAIGHT PINS + SCISSORS + ³/₄ YD (70CM) LACE TRIM + COORDINATING THREAD + SEWING MACHINE + APPROXIMATELY 2 YD (1.8M) RIBBON

PHOTO ON PAGE **34**

INSTRUCTIONS

1. Lay the sweater flat on your work surface with the front facing up. Use a safety pin to mark the front of the sweater. Mark a straight line across the sweater directly under both armholes. Cut the sweater on this line. You will only use the bottom part.

2. Try on the bottom part of the sweater, pulling it up over your chest and under your armpits. Make sure the marked front is facing front.

3. At the center front, pull the excess fabric away from your body until you have a tight fit. Mark this excess by pinning through both layers of fabric, starting at the top and going straight down. Remove the sweater carefully.

4. Cut off the excess fabric, following the marked line of pins to create the front opening of the corset.

5. Measure two pieces of lace trim to the length of the opening of the corset, adding ½" (13mm) seam allowance at both ends, and cut.

TIP AVOID FINE GAUGE SWEATERS FOR THIS PROJECT. CHUNKIER KNITS WITH BIGGER STITCHES PROVIDE FOR EASIER LACING OF THE RIBBON.

TIP ADD A CROCHETED EDGING FOR AN EVEN MORE UNIQUE LOOK.

VINTAGE TWIST USE A CONTRASTING RIBBON TO LACE UP YOUR CORSET AND REALLY MAKE IT POP, OR USE BUTTONS INSTEAD OF RIBBON FOR DIFFERENT LOOK.

TIP IF YOU ARE HAVING TROUBLE LACING THE RIBBON THROUGH THE KNITTED MATERIAL, SNIP SMALL HOLES AND REINFORCE THEM WITH EMBROIDERY FLOSS AND ZIGZAG STITCH.

6. Fold under the ends of one piece of lace trim ½" (13mm) at the top and bottom and place it along the edge of one side of the opening, folding under ½" (13mm) of trim to the wrong side. Pin into place and topstitch no more than ¼" (6mm) from the edge. Repeat for the other side of the opening.

7. Lay the corset flat with the center opening facing up. Use pins to mark the spots where the ribbon will be threaded on each side. With the ribbon folded in half, start at the bottom and begin threading the corset between the knit stitches where marked, as if you were lacing a shoe. Tie the ribbon in a bow at the top. Trim the ends if needed.

CAPELET

BUTTON-FRONT SKIRT + SCISSORS + **FULL A-LINE SKIRT** + RULER + TAILOR'S CHALK OR FABRIC PEN + COORDINATING THREAD + SEWING MACHINE + STRAIGHT PINS

PHOTO ON PAGE **37**

INSTRUCTIONS

1. Lay the button-front skirt flat on the work surface with the front facing up. Cut the shell from the skirt, leaving only the waistband and button placket. Leave a 1" (2.5cm) seam allowance under the waistband and on each side of the placket. Measure the length of the skirt from the top of the waist to the bottom of placket.

2. Lay the A-line skirt flat on the work surface with the front facing up. Starting at the bottom edge, measure and mark the length from the other skirt and add 1" (2.5cm). Cut straight across.

3. On the bottom section of the skirt you just cut, measure and mark a midpoint line on the front lengthwise. Cut the skirt open on this line.

4. Hand-sew a line of long stitches around the top edge of the skirt.

5. With right sides together, pin the right-hand side of the skirt to the right-hand side of the button placket, lining up the unfinished edges. Repeat for the left side of the skirt and button placket. Fold over the unfinished edge at the top of the skirt and pin to the waistband, gathering sections of fabric equally as you go, so the skirt will fit to the waistband.

6. On a sewing machine, zigzag stitch the skirt to the waistband and the button placket.

TIP MAKE SURE THE A-LINE SKIRT IS VERY FULL TO ACHIEVE THE CAPELET LOOK.

VINTAGE TWIST WANT A COLLAR? REMOVE ONE FROM A COAT OR ADD A VINTAGE FUR STOLE FROM A THRIFT SHOP.

KEEP IT OR CUT IT:
KNOWING YOUR DESIGNER VINTAGE

Technically, for *Born-Again Vintage* projects, I consider everything fair game. SEE IT, BUY IT, CUT IT, AND REMAKE IT—THAT'S MY MOTTO. But occasionally, you'll come across a piece that might make you think twice. Perhaps it's just a shade too perfect or in too great a shape to take fabric shears to it. The fact is you don't always have to deconstruct to achieve a born-again vintage feel.

So here's my standard rule of thumb: If you recognize the name of the designer as someone whose work is still valued today, consider it before chopping it up—whether or not you happen to like the look of the entire outfit. For example: You've come across a STRAPLESS KELLY-GREEN JIL SANDER DRESS FROM THE SEVENTIES. You love the bodice but hate the skirt; it's narrow and currently unfashionable. You can envision sewing a flowing new bottom onto the top and having a unique *Born-Again Vintage* item.

Stop. Don't do it.

IF IT FITS, IS IN GOOD CONDITION (free of stains or tears, not missing irreplaceable parts), KEEP IT INTACT AS PART OF YOUR PERSONAL VINTAGE COLLECTION. Styles change; you'll never know when this particular silhouette will come back into fashion. If it never does, or your figure changes, you can trade it back in at another consignment shop for something else.

Sometimes, even if you don't recognize the designer, or the piece is missing a label or is perhaps handmade, A GARMENT IS WORTH KEEPING INTACT IF YOU CAN USE IT AS A MODEL FOR FUTURE PROJECTS.

The point is there are no hard and fast rules. Don't feel required to take absolutely everything apart and reconstruct it with something else, even if, like me, that's your first instinct. And just because you find A TIMELESS VINTAGE PIECE doesn't mean you can't still make it your own without using the scissors. By simply removing the buttons and adding your own or removing the way-too-big shoulder pads, you've made a subtle change that KEEPS YOUR PIECE CLASSIC, BUT SLIGHTLY MORE "YOU." Not everything requires an extreme makeover.

That said, don't hesitate to take the best qualities of a piece of clothing and discard the rest, regardless of who made it. This is especially true when a stain appears permanent or the sleeves are an attractive length but the waist, well, it bulges. Trust me, it's not you and your "extra five pounds," it's the skirt and the way it's shaped. So use the sleeves for your born-again Cropped Jacket (page 98) and make the skirt into a throw pillow. YOU'LL FEEL A WHOLE LOT BETTER ABOUT YOURSELF AND GET SOME HOME DÉCOR IN THE BARGAIN.

T-SHIRT BLOUSE

VINTAGE BLOUSE + STRAIGHT PINS + TAILOR'S CHALK OR FABRIC PEN + SCISSORS + **FITTED KNIT T-SHIRT** + COORDINATING THREAD + SEWING MACHINE

PHOTO ON PAGE **38**

INSTRUCTIONS

1. Fold the unbuttoned vintage blouse so its left-hand neck seam lines up with its right-hand neck seam, and the left-hand side seam to the right-hand side seam, so that the right sides are facing. Pin in place.

2. Keeping the blouse folded, measure and mark a line that is $\frac{3}{8}$" (9mm) from the placket and then curves out to 1" (2.5cm) around the neck. Cut along this line.

3. Fold the fitted T-shirt in half lengthwise, with the front facing out. Pin away from the front fold to assure a precise cut.

4. Cut the T-shirt open on the center front fold, being careful not to cut the back.

5. With right sides together, pin the vintage blouse placket and collar into the fitted T-shirt by lining up the unfinished edges.

6. Sew the pieces together using a $\frac{1}{8}$" (3mm) seam allowance.

7. Finish the raw edges with a zigzag stitch or serger.

TIP DON'T THROW OUT THE SHELL OF THE BLOUSE. THERE ARE PLENTY OF USES FOR IT IF IT'S IN GOOD SHAPE (SEE BIB-FRONT TANK TOP, PAGE 104).

TIP THIS PROJECT IS PERFECT FOR A VINTAGE BLOUSE THAT HAS SHORT ARMS OR IS A BIT TOO WORN.

VINTAGE TWIST SUBSTITUTE THE FITTED T-SHIRT WITH A TANK TOP FOR A SUMMER LOOK.

PHOTO ON PAGE **41**

CROPPED JACKET

BROCADE COAT + TAILOR'S CHALK OR FABRIC PEN + SCISSORS + MEASURING TAPE OR RULER + STRAIGHT PINS + COORDINATING THREAD + SEWING MACHINE + 2½ YD (2.3M) MATCHING PIPING + 4 BUTTONS (1" [2.5CM] IN DIAMETER)

INSTRUCTIONS

1. Lay the coat flat on the work surface with the front facing up. Determine the desired length and shape. Mark with the chalk or fabric pen. Cut off straight across. If possible, cut 1" (2.5cm) beneath a button.

2. Determine the desired length of the sleeves and mark with the chalk or fabric pen. Cut off straight across.

3. Cut along the lengths of both side seams of the coat.

4. With the sleeves flat, cut along the top and bottom folds of each, starting from the cuff and stopping 2" (5cm) from shoulder.

5. Measure the length of the side seams of the coat. Using this measurement, cut triangle inserts from the excess fabric from the bottom of the coat, adding 1" (2.5cm) for seam allowances. The bottom of the triangles should be approximately 4–5" (10–13cm) wide including seam allowance. The widths are determined by how A-line you would like the jacket, but the inserts for each side should be identical.

VINTAGE TWIST INSTEAD OF USING PIPING AS THE TRIM, TRY LACE.

6. With the right sides together, pin the triangles into place in the opened side seams, making the necessary adjustments so the point at the top of each triangle is centered.

7. Sew the pieces together using a ¼" (6mm) seam allowance.

TIP IF THE COAT HAS A BELT, CUT IT TO CREATE EPAULETS FOR THE SHOULDERS (AS SHOWN).

8. Place the piping in the open seam along the bottom trim of the coat and pin; cut off the excess piping. Sew into place with the piping to the right of your needle and the needle positioned as far right as possible.

9. Measure the length of the cut on the sleeves. Using this measurement, cut triangle inserts from the excess fabric, adding 1" (2.5cm) for seam allowances. The bottom of the triangles should be approximately 6–7" (15–18cm) wide including seam allowance. The widths are determined by how wide you want your bell sleeves.

10. With right sides together, pin the triangles into place in the sleeve cuts, making the necessary adjustments so the point at the top of each triangle is centered.

11. Sew the pieces together, using a ¼" (6mm) seam allowance.

12. Finish the raw edges with a wide zigzag stitch, or use a serger.

13. If replacing the buttons, remove the old buttons and hand-sew new ones into place.

PHOTO ON PAGE **42**

WIDE BELT

BLAZER + TAILOR'S CHALK OR FABRIC PEN + SCISSORS + RULER + STRAIGHT PINS + COORDINATING THREAD + SEWING MACHINE

INSTRUCTIONS

1. Lay the blazer flat on the work surface. Measure and mark a line around the blazer 1" (2.5cm) above the second button at approximately waist level. Cut on this line.

2. Try this bottom piece on inside out, with the back facing front. Pull excess fabric away from your body until you have a snug fit. Mark this excess by pinning through both layers of the fabric, starting at the top and going straight down.

3. Remove the belt and cut off the excess fabric. Sew these raw edges together using a ¼" (6mm) seam allowance.

4. Fold over the top unfinished edge ½" (13mm) and topstitch.

TIP THE BELT SHOULD HAVE AT LEAST TWO BUTTONS AND NO MORE THAN THREE.

VINTAGE TWIST USE A PRETTY TRIM FOR EDGING OR ADD SOME OVERSIZED BUTTONS FOR DRAMATIC STATEMENT.

CHAPTER 3
SUMMER

PHOTO ON PAGE **46**

T-SHIRT DRESS

MEASURING TAPE OR RULER + **CAP-SLEEVE FITTED T-SHIRT** + TAILOR'S CHALK OR FABRIC PEN + SCISSORS + **VINTAGE DRESS** + STRAIGHT PINS + COORDINATING THREAD + SEWING MACHINE

INSTRUCTIONS

1. Measure the length from your collarbone to just beneath your bust. It should be approximately 12" (30.5cm). Lay the T-shirt flat on the work surface with the front facing up. Starting at the top, use that measurement to mark a line crosswise on the T-shirt. Cut the T-shirt along this line and set aside the top part. Save the bottom for another use or discard.

2. Lay the dress flat on the work surface with the front facing up. Starting from the bottom, measure and mark the desired length. Cut straight across on the marked line.

3. Turn the T-shirt inside out. Slip it over the bottom part of the dress, so that the right sides are together and the bottom edge of the T-shirt lines up with the top edge of the dress. Match any seams. Pin into place, stretching the T-shirt to fit the circumference of the dress. If it does not stretch to fit the dress, machine-sew a line of long stitches around the top edge of the dress. Pull the thread ends to create gathers and spread them evenly around the dress.

4. Machine-stitch the T-shirt to the dress with a ¼" (6mm) seam allowance. Remove the pins.

5. Finish the raw edge with a zigzag stitch, or use a serger.

TIP DON'T LET A DRESS WITH A ZIPPER SCARE YOU. YOU CAN JUST SEW ACROSS IT.

VINTAGE TWIST EXPERIMENT WITH THE LENGTH OF THE T-SHIRT. CUT IT SHORTER FOR A BABY-DOLL LOOK OR LEAVE IT LONGER TO ACCENTUATE THE WAISTLINE. THROW IN A VINTAGE BELT TO TIE IT ALL TOGETHER.

STRAPLESS TOP

**KNEE-LENGTH A-LINE SKIRT WITH AN ELASTIC WAISTBAND +
VINTAGE SCARF** OR **TIE** + TAILOR'S CHALK OR FABRIC PEN + RULER + SCISSORS

PHOTO ON PAGE **49**

INSTRUCTIONS

1. Lay the skirt flat on the work surface with the front facing up. Determine where you want the scarf or tie to be. This should be at least 1½" (3.8cm) from the bottom of the skirt.

2. Depending on the thickness of the scarf or the width of the tie, use the chalk or fabric pen to mark 1" (2.5cm) to 2" (5cm)-long slits, approximately 3" (7.5cm) to 5" (12.5cm) apart, around the skirt where you've placed the scarf or tie. The closer together the slits, the more gathered the top will be.

3. Cut open the slits and zigzag stitch around the edges to prevent fraying. Start weaving the scarf through the slits where you want it to tie, either the front, side, or back, until the two ends meet. Tie the ends in a knot or a bow.

TIP CREATE AN EMPIRE WAIST TOP BY CUTTING THE SLITS HIGHER SO THAT THE SCARF TIES UNDER THE BUST.

VINTAGE TWIST DON'T HESITATE TO USE A WINTER SKIRT FOR THIS PROJECT, BECAUSE THE TOP CAN EASILY MAKE THE TRANSITION INTO FALL WHEN WORN WITH A BLAZER OR SHRUG. WEAR WITH SKINNY JEANS FOR A BALANCED SILHOUETTE.

PHOTO ON PAGE **50**

BIB-FRONT TANK TOP

VINTAGE BLOUSE + SCISSORS + TAILOR'S CHALK OR FABRIC PEN + STRAIGHT PINS +
TANK TOP + SEWING MACHINE + COORDINATING THREAD

INSTRUCTIONS

1. Lay the vintage blouse flat on the work surface with the front facing up. Cut off the sleeves of the blouse at the shoulder seams.

2. With the blouse buttoned up, fold it in half lengthwise, with the front facing out. Mark the center front and back with the chalk or fabric pen.

3. With the shoulder seams of the blouse aligned, pin into place.

4. Mark the desired shape on the blouse with the chalk or fabric pen. Add a ½" (13mm) seam allowance on the outside of all markings.

5. Cut and remove the marked section from the vintage blouse.

6. Cut and remove the binding from the neck of the tank top.

7. Fold the tank top in half lengthwise, with the front facing out, and mark the center front and back with the chalk or fabric pen.

8. Place the vintage blouse piece on top of the tank top, lining up the center front and back marks.

VINTAGE TWIST IF USING A PRINTED TANK TOP, BE SURE YOUR COLORS COMPLEMENT EACH OTHER.

9. Fold the edges under so right sides are together. Pin the pieces together securely.

TIP USE A PRINT OR COLORED TANK TOP.

10. Add a ½" (13mm) seam allowance and then cut away the fabric of the tank top where the vintage blouse section will be inserted. Remove the pins.

11. Now with the right sides together, pin the bib and the tank top in place. Machine-stitch using a ½" (13mm) seam allowance.

12. Trim all seams to ¼" (6mm), and finish using a narrow zigzag stitch or serger.

VINTAGE PATTERNS
AND REPRODUCTION FABRICS

IN THE ANTIQUE WORLD, the word "reproduction" is often accompanied by a shudder. However, *Born-Again Vintage* is not above trying just about anything to get the look you want—even if that means a reproduction here or there.

Basically, THERE ARE TWO WAYS TO ACHIEVE A VERY HONEST RETRO LOOK without shopping in vintage boutiques for finished pieces. You can either find a vintage pattern and use a modern fabric to make part or all of it. Or you can USE A MODERN PATTERN WITH A REPRODUCED VINTAGE FABRIC. Either way, you'll probably have to do some Web research or troll around some antique stores. But sooner or later, you will wind up with the materials to help you achieve your goal.

For instance, Woodland Farms Vintage (see Helpful Websites, page 133, for all of the sites discussed here) has more than 1,000 PATTERNS FROM THE VICTORIAN ERA TO 1960 in stock, boasting such names as *Butterick, Ladies' Home Journal*, Marquardt's, *McCall, Vogue, Woman's Home,* and many more. Not only that, but the site also carries VINTAGE TEXTILES AND MAGAZINES, so you can make an authentic item from start to finish according to your own contemporary measurements.

As far as reproduced vintage fabrics go, at places like Reprodepot Fabrics, some of the mostly all-cotton designs are direct reproductions, while others are inspired by them. Or take a look at Ruby Jane's Retro Fabric and More, which has a variety of textures (wool and muslin, for instance), as well as patterns for linens and bedding so YOU CAN EXTEND YOUR *Born-Again Vintage* EXPERTISE TO THE HOME.

DENIM BAG

1 PAIR OF VINTAGE JEANS + SCISSORS + TAILOR'S CHALK OR FABRIC PEN + RULER + COORDINATING THREAD + SEWING MACHINE + STRAIGHT PINS + **VINTAGE CANVAS BELT** + 18" (45.5CM) X 10" (25.5CM) **FABRIC OF YOUR CHOICE** + EMBROIDERY NEEDLE + EMBROIDERY FLOSS (8MM) + LARGE BUTTON (OPTIONAL) + SELF-ADHESIVE VELCRO PATCHES (OPTIONAL)

PHOTO ON PAGE 53

BAG

1. Lay the jeans flat on the work surface with the front facing up. Cut straight across above the crotch.

2. With the top of the jeans on your work surface, turn one pant leg horizontally and line it up with the bottom of the top section. Mark the width of the top section on the pant leg. Mark and add a ½" (13mm) seam allowance to each side. Cut the pant leg with each side slightly flaring out at the bottom.

3. Cut the (in)seam off at the top of the pant leg.

4. With the right sides of the pant leg together, machine-stitch the side seams using a ½" (13mm) seam allowance.

5. With the right sides together, pin the pant leg to the top section of the jeans, lining up the unfinished edges. Pin into place.

6. Machine-stitch using a ¼" (6mm) seam allowance. Turn the right side out and press, if necessary.

VINTAGE TWIST INSTEAD OF USING A LARGE BUTTON FOR THE CLOSURE, USE A BROOCH OR SMALL BELT BUCKLE. BE CREATIVE!

7. The canvas belt will be used as your bag strap. Remove any hardware. Determine how long you would like the strap to be, then mark it and cut.

8. Place the strap on the inside of each waistband side seam and pin in place.

TIP IF YOU WANT A MEDIUM-SIZE BAG, CUT THE PANT LEG IN HALF HORIZONTALLY. IF YOU WANT A SMALL BAG, USE ONLY THE TOP OF THE JEANS.

9. Machine-sew an X and then a square around the X at each end of the strap to attach it to the waistband.

FLAP

1. Cut the other pant leg open at one of the seams. Then cut an 18" (45.5cm) x 10" (25.5cm) section.

2. Cut a piece of the fabric with the same measurements.

3. With the right sides together, topstitch around the edges, leaving one long side open.

4. Turn the right side out and topstitch the flap closed.

5. Pin ¼" (6mm) of the edge of the flap to the inside of the bag at the back waistband. Make sure the contrasting fabric is showing on the front of the bag.

6. Using the embroidery needle and embroidery floss, hand-sew the flap from the inside of the bag. The thread should not show on the outside of the bag.

CLOSURE (OPTIONAL)

1. Place a large button halfway down on the center bottom of the flap. Sew into place.

2. On the underside of the flap, place Velcro patches on each corner. Place corresponding patches on the body of the bag.

SHORT SHORTS

ELASTIC WAIST A-LINE VINTAGE SKIRT + MEASURING TAPE +
COORDINATING THREAD + MARKING PENCIL + SCISSORS

INSTRUCTIONS

PHOTO ON PAGE **54**

1. Lay the skirt on the work surface facing up. Using a measuring tape, measure from your waist to the top of your inseam (start at your navel for a low waist) or measure the rise of your favorite pants for an assured fit.

2. Mark your measurement on the skirt, making a mark in the center of skirt.

3. After determining where the top of the inseam, determine what length you want your shorts from the marked center. Mark and add ½" (13mm) for seam allowance.

4. Cut straight across at the marked length from side seam to side seam.

5. Fold the skirt in half, creating a center fold from waist to hem.

6. Cut from the marked center, cutting slightly upward toward the edge.

TIP WHILE VINTAGE PLAID MIGHT SEEM LIKE A FABULOUS IDEA, IT CAN BE UNCOMFORTABLE TO WEAR. BE SURE TO CHOOSE A COMFORTABLE FABRIC!

7. To check that the shorts will fit your leg, place a folded pair of your own fitted pants on top of the folded skirt and mark the width. Don't cut beyond marked width.

8. When unfolded, the skirt shape should resemble an upside down "U."

VINTAGE TWIST ADD A WIDE BELT TO THESE SHORTS TO CREATE A MODERN COMBO.

9. Turn the skirt inside out and machine-stitch the inseam, leaving ½" (13mm) for seam allowance.

10. Stitch again 1/4" (6mm) from previous stitch to create a secure inseam.

11. Finish the edges with a serger or wide zigzag stitch.

12. Turn the shorts right side out and hem the legs, folding up the raw edge 1/2" (13mm) and topstitching down.

PATTERNS

CHAPTER 4
FALL

PHOTO ON PAGE **58**

MINI-PONCHO

PULLOVER MEN'S OR **WOMEN'S SWEATER**, 1 SIZE LARGER THAN YOUR NORMAL SIZE FOR AN AVERAGE FIT, OR 2 SIZES LARGER FOR AN OVERSIZE FIT + SCISSORS + CROCHET HOOK, 4MM OR LARGER; COORDINATING YARN OR SEWING MACHINE; COORDINATING THREAD

INSTRUCTIONS

TIP IF YOU CUT YOUR SWEATER AND IT'S TOO LONG, IT BECOMES A TYPICAL PONCHO; TOO SHORT, AND YOU'VE GOT YOURSELF AN OLD-FASHIONED DICKIE. BE SURE TO TRY THE SWEATER ON BEFORE YOU CUT.

1. Using a different-colored basting thread or yarn, measure and mark a line around the sweater just above the armhole and slightly higher at each shoulder.

2. Cut the sweater just below the basting line.

3. If you choose not to crochet, skip to the instructions below for reinforcing the edges. Using the crochet hook and the unraveled yarn from the body of the sweater, or yarn of your choice, work a round of slip stitch around the circumference of the piece just above the basting line. Do not break the yarn.

4. Work a round of single crochet on top of the slip stitch edging. Remove the basting thread. For a firmer edge, work one half-double-crochet row above the single crochet row.

TIP USE UNRAVELED YARN FROM THE UNUSED PORTION OF THE SWEATER TO FINISH THE RAW EDGES.

OR

Using your sewing machine and a wide zigzag stitch, sew along the cut edge of the piece. Repeat one more time to prevent fraying.

VINTAGE TWIST CUSTOMIZE THE NECKLINE BY CUTTING A BOATNECK IF YOU WANT TO ADD AN EXTRA SPARK.

HIGH-WAISTED SKIRT

MINI DRESS (HEAVIER FABRICS SUCH AS POLYESTER GIVE A MORE STRUCTURED LOOK) + TAILOR'S CHALK OR FABRIC PEN + RULER + SCISSORS + **RIBBED SWEATER** OR TOP (COTTON WORKS WELL) + STRAIGHT PINS + SEWING MACHINE + COORDINATING THREAD + 6 BUTTONS (OPTIONAL)

PHOTO ON PAGE **61**

INSTRUCTIONS

1. Lay the dress flat on the work surface with the front facing up. Determine the desired length of the skirt from hip to hem and use the chalk or fabric pen and a ruler to mark a straight line. Keep in mind that the total length of the skirt also includes the bottom portion of the sweater, approximately 5" to 6" (12.5cm to 15cm). Cut the marked section of the dress off. Set it aside.

2. Lay the sweater or top flat on the work surface with the front facing up. Measure and mark a straight line 2" (5cm) above the ribbed hem. Cut the marked section off the sweater.

3. With the right sides together, line up the edges of the top of the sweater and the top of the skirt. Pin into place.

4. Using a ¼" (6mm) seam allowance, machine-stitch the sweater to the skirt. Finish the raw edge with a zigzag stitch, or use a serger. Remove the pins.

5. Fold the sweater section up and lightly press the new seam with an iron, if necessary.

6. Sew the buttons on as illustrated in the photo, if desired.

TIP CHOOSE A SWEATER OR TOP MADE WITH A SOFT FABRIC. THOUGH YOU MAY BE ATTRACTED TO THE COLOR OF A PARTICULAR WOOL SWEATER, IT MAY NOT FEEL SO NICE AGAINST YOUR SKIN.

VINTAGE TWIST PULL ON SOME SUSPENDERS AND GET READY TO STRUT THE CATWALK!

SHOW ME THE SHOES AND PURSES

Matching a *Born-Again Vintage* piece with an authentic shoe or purse from the era you've based your garment on is a personal choice. Say you've completed the Winter Vest (page 22) and you want A SEVENTIES LACE-UP KNEE-HIGH BOOT made in spats style to go with the look. Search the Web and no doubt you can find a pair, or something similar.

I suggest, however, that you approach your shoes and purses with an eye toward rehabbing them, too. Take out the existing boot laces and put in BLACK SILK RIBBONS THAT SUGGEST VAMPY NEW YORK OR CHICAGO NIGHTS. Replace the strap of a messenger bag from the 1960s with the wide belt of a 1940s shirtdress, or use the buckle as a fastener. Clip a pair of YOUR GREAT-GRANDMOTHER'S RHINESTONE EARRINGS on black suede slingbacks from the 1950s.

Or you can start modern with a pair of pumps or a clutch from your favorite store and turn them into ONE-OF-A-KIND ITEMS with the addition of seed pearl or beaded appliqués. As with all *Born-Again Vintage* projects, you'll still need the basic materials. IT'S WHAT YOU DO WITH THEM THAT WILL MAKE THE DIFFERENCE.

SWEATER HOODIE

KNIT SWEATER + STRAIGHT PINS + SCISSORS + HOODED JACKET OR SWEATSHIRT WITH FRONT ZIPPER AND POCKETS + TAILOR'S CHALK OR FABRIC PEN + COORDINATING THREAD + SEWING MACHINE

INSTRUCTIONS

1. Fold the sweater in half lengthwise, with the front facing out. With the shoulder and the side seams aligned, pin the sweater into place.

2. Cut on the center fold on the front only. Remove pins and set aside.

3. Lay the jacket flat on the work surface with the front facing up. Use chalk to mark a 1½" (3.8cm) seam allowance around the ribbed waistband, pockets, zipper placket, and hood. Cut and remove these sections in one piece.

4. Lay the sweater flat on the work surface. With the jacket piece zipped up, carefully pin it to the sweater. Cut the sweater neck, if necessary, to fit the shape of the jacket neck.

5. With the seam allowance of the jacket piece folded under ½" (13mm), topstitch the ribbed waistband, inner pocket layers, and zipper placket to the sweater.

6. For the neck, turn the two pieces inside out so that the right sides are together and line up the unfinished edges of the jacket and sweater necks. Pin into place. Machine-stitch using a ½" (13mm) seam allowance.

7. Finish all the edges with a zigzag stitch, or use a serger, to prevent fraying.

PHOTO ON PAGE **63**

TIP BE SURE THE SIZES OF THE JACKET AND THE SWEATER ARE EQUIVALENT.

VINTAGE TWIST FOR THIS PROJECT, SIMPLE WORKS BEST. USE A SOLID-COLOR HOODIE WITH A CASHMERE SWEATER OF A COORDINATING COLOR, AND YOU HAVE A HOODIE TO DIE FOR!

PHOTO ON PAGE **64**

VINTAGE COMBO DRESS

1 VINTAGE PRINT DRESS + 1 SOLID-COLORED DRESS (HEAVY WOOL OR TWEED WORKS BEST) + RULER OR TAPE MEASURE + TAILOR'S CHALK OR FABRIC PEN + SCISSORS + SEAM RIPPER + COORDINATING THREAD + SEWING MACHINE + STRAIGHT PINS

INSTRUCTIONS

1. Determine which top half and which bottom half of each of the dresses you will be using.

2. Measure from your shoulder to your waist. On the dress you are using for the top half of this project, measure and mark this shoulder-to-waist measurement, adding an extra 1" (2.5cm) for the seam allowance. Cut the top half of the dress off, cutting around the zipper (if one exists).

3. Using a seam ripper, remove the sleeves. Fold the existing seam allowance under and topstitch the edges around the armholes for a finished hem. Skip to step 6 if neither dress has zippers.

4. Using a seam ripper, take the zipper (if applicable) out of the dress that you are using for the bottom half of the project. Discard the zipper or save it for a future project.

5. Measure the length of zipper sticking out from the bottom of the top half of the dress. Mark this measurement, plus a 1" (2.5cm) seam allowance, on the bottom half of the dress.

VINTAGE TWIST KEEP THE TOP HALF OF THE DRESS YOU DIDN'T USE FOR THE CROPPED JACKET (PAGE 98).

6. Cut the bottom half of the dress you will be using. If unsure how much to cut off, your waist to shoulder measurements should be your guide.

TIP LOOK FOR DRESSES WITH INTERESTING COLLARS, PRINTS, AND TEXTURES. DRESS COATS WORK FOR THIS PROJECT, TOO.

7. Note: If neither dress has a zipper, proceed with the instructions and ignore all zipper directions. If the bottom half of the dress does not have a zipper, sew in the zipper from the top of the dress to the bottom dress by topstitching both sides and the bottom of the zipper into the back seam, or vice versa if the top of the dress has no zipper but the bottom dress does.

8. Sew the top and bottom halves of the dresses together by matching the unfinished edges with the right sides facing, starting at one side of the zipper, and machine-stitch until you meet other side of the zipper. If there are no zippers, machine-stitch straight around.

9. If one of the dresses has a contrasting collar, you can sew it to the new bodice. Using a seam ripper, carefully remove the collar from the dress top.

10. Position the collar so that the opening is at the center front of the bodice. Pin into place.

11. Topstitch the dress neck to the top of the collar. Finish all of the raw edges with a zigzag stitch, or use a serger.

FEELING FOR FABRIC:
REVIVAL TEXTILES AT FAIR-TRADE PRICES

When looking for VINTAGE FABRIC FOR YOUR BORN-AGAIN DESIGNS, don't assume all you need to know is all that meets your eye. Sure, you can tell what's wool or cotton or satin or even taffeta at a glance—you probably don't even have to touch it to confirm. And IF YOU'RE CRAFTY TO BEGIN WITH, you know your dimity from your Swiss dot.

But can you date your fabrics? Can you estimate their weight? And given both of those things, can you then surmise about how much they should cost per yard—and whether buying a particular dress or skirt for its fabric alone makes monetary sense?

In general, for LIGHTWEIGHT FLOCKED OR SWISS-DOTTED COTTON AND SEMI-SHEER FABRICS FROM THE 1920S TO THE 1960S, you should be paying an average of $12 to $15 per yard. For rayon from the same era, estimate about $18 to $20 per yard. Prices go way up for silks, chiffons, and brocades: from $25 to $40 per yard. So buying A VINTAGE CHIFFON GOWN for $80 or $100 might not be such a bad deal after all—if it has a very full skirt.

The bottom line is if you feel like you're paying too much for a single item, you probably are.

If you want to "fill in" your projects—suppose you need to add front and back panels to a skirt—and don't feel like messing around by taking apart another garment, some websites sell ORIGINAL VINTAGE FABRIC AT FAIR PRICES. Sometimes, for the Halter Dress (page 130), all you need is a yard or two for the inserts to complete the piece. However, due to the rarity of some of these fabrics, you might need to buy a certain amount—a minimum or maximum yardage. So this proposition can be expensive, too.

One way to save money is to SHARE MATERIALS WITH A FIBER-HAPPY FRIEND, as long as you coordinate your outfits so that you don't wear them on the same day. Buying reproduction fabrics is another, less expensive way to go. For both ORIGINAL VINTAGE AND REPRODUCTION FABRIC websites, see Helpful Resources (page 133).

PHOTO ON PAGE **66**

ARM WARMERS

SWEATER SLEEVES + SCISSORS + EMBROIDERY NEEDLE + EMBROIDERY FLOSS (8MM OR LESS) + SEWING MACHINE + COORDINATING THREAD + RULER + NEEDLE + COORDINATING YARN + CROCHET NEEDLE

INSTRUCTIONS

1. Use the sweater sleeves from a previous project in this book (such as Sweater Corset, page 93), or cut off the sleeves from another sweater. Place the sleeves on top of each other, lining up cuff ends and seams.

2. Cut the tops of the sleeves straight across to create even edges and ensure they are equal in length.

3. You have 3 options for finishing the raw edges: crochet finish using a standard running stitch; fold over the top edges ¼" (6mm) and topstitch with a sewing machine; or fold over the top edges ¼" (6mm) and topstitch using hand-embroidery.

4. To make the thumbholes, measure 1½" (3.8cm) from the finished edges and cut 1" (2.5cm) slits along the inseams.

5. To finish the thumbhole opening, crochet an edging or hand-embroider.

TIP WHEN IT COMES TO THE SWEATER SLEEVE, THE TIGHTER THE BETTER, BECAUSE YOU'LL WANT YOUR ARM WARMER TO STAY UP.

VINTAGE TWIST WEAR ARM WARMERS OVER TOP OF A FITTED, LONG-SLEEVED T-SHIRT FOR A FUNKY LAYERED LOOK.

CHAPTER 5

PRETTY IN A BLINK

STRAPLESS MINI-DRESS

VINTAGE DRESS + SCISSORS + STRAIGHT PINS + TAILOR'S CHALK OR FABRIC PEN + COORDINATING THREAD + SEWING MACHINE + MEASURING TAPE OR RULER + 1 YD (91CM) ELASTIC, ¼" (6MM) WIDE + 2 YD (1.8M) COORDINATING RIBBON

PHOTO ON PAGE **70**

INSTRUCTIONS

1. Lay the dress flat on the work surface with the front facing up. Cut off the sleeves.

2. Fold the dress in half lengthwise, with the front facing out. Align side seams and pin.

3. Using chalk, mark the desired shape for the top front of the dress, blending in to the bottom of the armhole. Cut, and remove pins.

4. Fold the dress in half lengthwise again, this time with the back facing out, and pin into place. Mark the desired shape for the back, blending in to meet the bottom of the armhole. Be sure to make the back lower than the front. Cut, and remove pins.

5. Finish the neckline by folding the unfinished edges down ¼" (6mm), so the wrong sides are together. Lightly press. Fold down the edge another ¼" (6mm). Press and pin into place. Topstitch the hem close to the edge.

TIP PROM DRESSES AND BRIDESMAID'S DRESSES WORK GREAT

VINTAGE TWIST EMBELLISHMENTS SUCH AS RHINESTONES OR PEARLS REMOVED FROM THE DRESS CAN BECOME EARRINGS OR A HAIR CLIP.

6. Try on the dress and mark your desired length with chalk. Remove the excess fabric from the bottom of the dress, leaving the lining intact. If the dress has tiers, remove all but the bottom tier with scissors.

TIP SEW THE LEFTOVER FABRIC TOGETHER TO CREATE A MATCHING SHAWL OR SHRUG.

7. Fold the lining up to match the new length of the dress, and leaving a ¼" (6mm) seam allowance, cut off any excess. Hem the lining by folding the unfinished edges under ¼" (6mm), pinning into place, and topstitching close to the edge

8. Try on the dress and measure from the top of the dress to under the chest, adding an additional 1½" (4cm), and mark using pins.

9. Remove the dress. Following the marks made with pins, pin around circumference of dress, making sure you have an even line from front to back.

10. Starting ½" (13mm) from the zipper (if the dress has one), take the elastic and, using a wide zigzag stitch, sew it to the dress directly above the pin line on the wrong side of the fabric. Backstitch a few times at the start and finish of the elastic for reinforcement. Remove the pins.

11. Place the top of the ribbon directly above the elastic line on the front of the dress and pin into place. Using a topstitch, begin sewing at the center of the back, stretching the dress as you go. Repeat for the bottom of the ribbon.

TO GLOVE OR NOT TO GLOVE

Let's face it: EVENING GLOVES ARE A TEMPTATION. They're the apples of the vintage garden. Long or short, satin or crocheted, buttoned or fingerless, they're tough to resist, and you can end up with a drawerfull. And we never wear them. Why? Because THEY'RE SILKY, SOFT, SOPHISTI-CATED, AND THEY ALWAYS LOOK SO GOOD—on someone else for a fancy occasion we might never happen upon.

Okay, it's not all that bad. Actually, evening gloves sometimes do look really great with born again projects such as the Strapless Mini-dress (page 121). When so much flesh shows, adding long, pearl-button, CHAMPAGNE-COLORED GLOVES FROM 1910 or wrist-length, white, embroidered, KID LEATHER EVENING GLOVES FROM THE 1930S is extra sexy. Or something like MOD 1960S DRIVING GLOVES, in shiny ivory and trimmed with black, is a terrific accessory for the Winter Vest (page 22).

But there are other CLEVER IDEAS FOR GLOVES. An extra long one can tie around the brim of a hat. A particularly decorative one can be draped around the neck on a sweater—perhaps sewn on that way with the hands crossed over the "heart." A pair of loosely gathered, elbow-length, nylon, chartreuse gloves WOULD BE AWESOME AS MATERIALS FOR ARM WARMERS (page 66), once the fingers are cut off.

Or you can just keep on making Pretty in a Blink dresses to match all those gloves you already have. That's the kind of solution I also tend to like.

PHOTO ON PAGE **73**

VINTAGE JUMPER

VINTAGE GOWN + MEASURING TAPE OR RULER + TAILOR'S CHALK OR FABRIC PEN + SCISSORS + STRAIGHT PINS + COORDINATING THREAD + SEWING MACHINE + ½ YD (45.5CM) OF MATCHING FABRIC + SEWING NEEDLE + 2½ YD (2.3M) COORDINATING TRIM (GIMPS OR ANY FLAT TRIM WORKS WELL)

INSTRUCTIONS

1. Lay the dress flat on the work surface with the front facing up. Determine the desired length of the dress and mark it with the chalk or fabric pen, leaving 1" (2.5cm) for the seam allowance and hem.

2. Cut straight across along the line.

3. Finish the hem of the dress by folding up the unfinished edge ½" (13mm), so the wrong sides are together. Lightly press. Fold the edge up another ½" (13mm). Press and pin into place.

4. Topstitch the hem close to the edge.

5. If the dress has a lining, cut if off along the edge of the new hem, and repeat steps 3 and 4.

6. Lay the dress flat again and mark the new shape of the neck leaving a ¼" (6mm) seam allowance. Cut where it is marked.

VINTAGE TWIST THE FABRIC CUT FROM THE BOTTOM WILL MAKE A PERFECT MATCHING CLUTCH. FIND A PATTERN ON ONE OF THE HELPFUL RESOURCES (PAGE 133).

7. Finish the neckline edges by folding down the unfinished edge
   ½" (13mm), so the wrong sides are together. Lightly press. Fold
   down the edge another ½" (13mm). Press and pin into place.

8. Topstitch the hem close to the edge.

9. Lay the dress flat on your work table so the front is facing up.
   Measure 2" (5cm) down from waistline and 1½" (4cm) from the
   side seam and mark. Measure 6" (15cm) down from that mark
   and make another mark. Repeat for other side.

10. Cut a slit between each mark, being careful not to cut the lining
    (if applicable).

    TIP ADD THE PERFECT VINTAGE
    TOUCH USING A BROOCH OR HAIR PIN.

11. With ½ yd (45.5m) of matching fabric folded in half, mark the
    outline for 2 pockets (using a pocket from an old garment as
    your pattern or outline), making sure the width is the same
    measurement as the slits you made and adding an extra ½"
    (13mm) for the seam allowance. Cut out the pockets.

12. Sew the pockets together with the right sides facing each other,
    making sure the opening stays open.

13. Take a pocket and place it inside one of the slits, matching the
    top edge to the front of the slit and the bottom edge to the back
    of the slit. Pin into place.

14. Fold the raw edges of the piece and the slit opening down so
    their right sides are facing. Hand-sew the pocket piece to the
    dress. Repeat with the other pocket.

15. Hand-sew the coordinating trim to the neckline, waist, and
    pocket edges.

PHOTO ON PAGE **74**

REMIX DRESS

SUMMER DRESS + MEASURING TAPE OR RULER + 1 YD (91CM) OF CROCHETED FABRIC OR CROCHETED BLANKET + SCISSORS + STRAIGHT PINS + COORDINATING THREAD + SEWING MACHINE + TAPESTRY OR CHENILLE NEEDLE (OPTIONAL) + COORDINATING EMBROIDERY FLOSS (OPTIONAL)

INSTRUCTIONS

1. Lay the dress flat on the work surface with the front facing up. Measure the width of the dress from side seam to side seam, adding 1" (2.5cm) on both sides for seam allowances.

2. Measure the length from the top of the dress to the waist, adding 1" (2.5cm) at both ends for seam allowances.

3. Using these length and width measurements, cut the crocheted piece to match.

4. Cut fabric from the front of the bodice if it's too bulky, leaving ½" (13mm) for the seam allowance.

5. Place the crocheted piece on top of the dress, matching the edges so all sides fit perfectly, turning over the edges of the crochet piece if necessary to match. Pin the piece to the dress.

6. Topstitch the piece into place. If the dress has boning in the bodice, then you must hand-sew the piece to the dress.

VINTAGE TWIST EXPERIMENT WITH A VARIETY OF FABRICS BEFORE YOU SEW. AUDITION SILKS, SUEDES, AND HAND KNITS UNTIL YOU FIND THE RIGHT LOOK FOR YOU.

7. (Optional) Make a matching bolero using leftover fabric. Cut the fabric into a long rectangle about 6" (15cm) wider than the width of your shoulders and about 12" (30.5cm) from top to bottom. Fold the rectangle in half lengthwise. Using a tapestry needle and coordinating embroidery floss, hand-sew 3" (7.5cm) together on each end of the open side. These will be the arm-holes. Whipstitch around all raw edges to finish the look.

TIP IF YOU ARE USING CROCHETED GRANNY SQUARES, PLAY WITH THEIR POSITIONING TO CREATE AN INTERESTING NECKLINE.

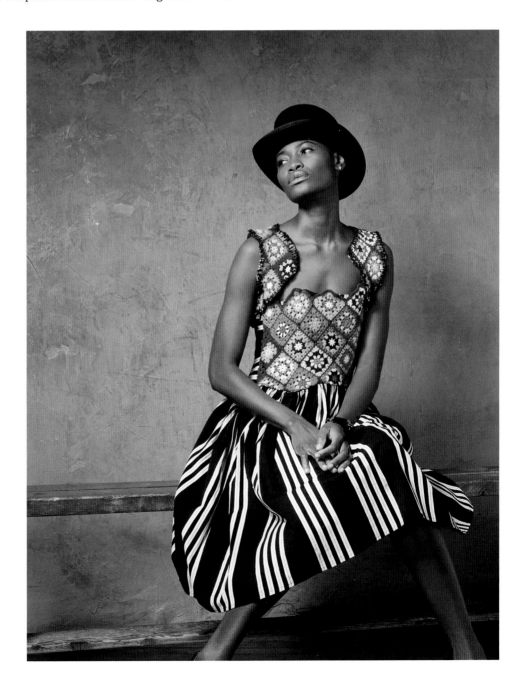

TOPPING IT:
HINTS ABOUT HATS

VINTAGE HATS tend to be elaborate and for that reason alone are hard to wear, especially if you've already got on another period item or two. Plus, many hats designed in the thirties and forties were designed to be worn over certain hairstyles, BUNS, AND EVEN BEEHIVES, and have inside crowns that you might find oddly sized—unless, of course, you happen to have a very small head.

Frankly, I think THE BEST THINGS ABOUT VINTAGE HATS ARE THE EMBELLISHMENTS! You can snag some real treasures here: Peacock and ostrich feathers dyed in a whole rainbow of colors (I've even seen real, scavenged wings and faux whole birds as decorations). SILK RIBBONS AND BLACK LACE. Velvet rosettes and bows. SILVER, GOLD, OR RED LAMÉ CORD. Flowers galore. Add these to your sewing bag for future projects.

Naturally, my inclination is to strip the hats bare and give them a whole new look. By keeping their basic materials and updating their crowns with the latest in scarves and head wraps, or even a cool vintage belt from another project's skirt or dress, YOU CAN CREATE A WHOLE NEW LOOK THAT INCORPORATES A NOD TO FASHION ERAS GONE BY. With sturdy leather and some felt hats, you can also try changing the shape into something more mod by steaming it over a teakettle and gently bending. Just mold the hat with your fingers as it gets soft from the steam, then let it sit to dry in the shape you've created.

There is one type of hat I will cut up and use for trim: THE FIFTIES FUR TOQUE, which is a close-fitting brimless hat, and, if you can find one, a matching muff. I'd certainly never go out and buy a modern-day pelt, so buying and refashioning vintage furs is a great way to RECYCLE WHAT ALREADY EXISTS. You can get the absolutely luscious look of fur while maintaining a clear conscience.

I do have one standard rule of thumb, however. Should you come across a classic hat that fits you perfectly—say, a 1920S FLAPPER CLOCHE or a BEATNIK 1960S BERET—don't change a thing. These hats go in and out of style on a regular basis, and you'll be delighted that you own AN AUTHENTIC ARTICLE WHEN IT'S TRENDY once again.

PHOTO ON PAGE **76**

HALTER DRESS

1¹/₂ YD (1.4M) OF COORDINATING FABRIC + RULER + TAILOR'S CHALK
OR FABRIC PEN + SCISSORS + COORDINATING THREAD + SEWING MACHINE +
VINTAGE DRESS WITH PRINCESS SEAMS AND HIGH NECK +
STRAIGHT PINS + SEAM RIPPER

INSTRUCTIONS

1. Fold the 1½ yd (1.4m) of fabric in half lengthwise.

2. Measure and mark two godets, or inserts, on the folded fabric. The godets should measure 2" (5cm) wide at the top, 17" (43cm) long, and 7" (18cm) wide at the bottom. (This includes a ½" [13mm] seam allowance.)

3. Cut out the 2 shapes. There will be a total of 4 inserts, since the fabric was folded.

4. Fold under the bottom of the inserts ¼" (6mm) so the wrong sides are together and lightly press. Fold under again ¼" (6mm) and press. Machine-stitch the hem at the bottom of the inserts.

5. Lay the dress flat on your work surface with the front facing up. At each side seam, measure and mark a line 16" (40.5cm) from the bottom of the dress and cut straight up.

6. Repeat at the back princess seams.

VINTAGE TWIST USE THE FABRIC THAT WAS REMOVED FROM THE BACK FOR A VARIATION ON THE DENIM BAG (PAGE 107) TO COMPLEMENT YOUR NEW DRESS.

7. With the right sides together, match the unfinished edges of the insert with the one of the cuts in the dress. Pin into place.

8. Machine-stitch each side of the insert to the dress, starting at the hem and using a ½" (13mm) seam allowance. Repeat for the remaining inserts. Remove the pins.

TIP FOR A FULLER SKIRT, USE MORE INSERTS.

9. To create the halter, first open the shoulder seams and carefully remove the back of the bodice from the collar with a seam ripper. Re-hem the back of the collar by folding the raw edge under and topstitching close to the edge.

10. Determine how low you want the back of the dress to be and mark it at the center back. From there, work outward to mark the whole shape of the back cut-out. Start cutting from the mark at the center back and cut up to each armhole.

11. To shape the front of the dress, measure and mark a 1" (2.5cm) width from both sides of the neckline toward the shoulders and cut diagonally down to the armholes.

12. Turn down the unfinished edges ¼" (6mm) on the front and back bodices and topstitch close to the edge to finish the hems.

HELPFUL RESOURCES

When looking for odds and ends, or even original vintage pieces, to complete your projects, don't overlook the big chain stores and consignment or thrift franchises. Sure, it's fun to go digging at the local church/synagogue thrift shop or find a forgotten treasure at a neighboring estate sale, but when searching for that perfect button, lace trim, or really cool tank top, the have-everything emporiums (or, in the case of the buy-sell-trade stores, the have-whatevers) really are a no-brainer. And they don't make your outfits appear any less authentic. Here are some of the national stores I depend on. Check the websites for a location near you:

A.C. MOORE
Arts & Crafts
866-342-8802
www.acmoore.com

BUFFALO EXCHANGE
New and Recycled Fashion
520-622-2711
www.buffaloexchange.com

THE CLOTHING WAREHOUSE
Classic Vintage
404-766-3432
www.theclothingwarehouse.com

CROSSROADS TRADING CO.
Buy-Sell-Trade Clothing/ Recycled Fashion
510-843-7600
www.crossroadstrading.com

GOODWILL INDUSTRIES
800-741-0186
www.goodwill.org

JO-ANN
Fabric and Craft Stores
888-739-4120
www.joann.com/joann

MICHAELS
Arts, Crafts & More
800-642-4235
www.michaels.com

NEARLY NEW SHOPS
The Association of Junior Leagues International
404-355-3547
www.ajli.org

OUT OF THE CLOSET
Thrift Stores
877-274-2548
www.outofthecloset.org

PLATO'S CLOSET
Gently Used Brand Name Clothing
800-567-6600
www.platoscloset.com

THE SALVATION ARMY
615 Slaters Lane
P.O. Box 269
Alexandria, VA 22313
www.salvationarmyusa.org

VINTAGE OUTFITTERS—
A STATE-BY-STATE DIRECTORY

As for indie vintage, thrift, and consignment boutiques, the following caught my eye for various reasons. But this is by no means an exhaustive list. If I could, I'd rent a U-Haul and go vintage shopping across the country just to supply you with such a list! Failing that, I like to pop into retro and secondhand shops whenever I can on my travels, whether they're real (like my trip to sell my line at a show in Miami) or virtual (like a journey on the Internet to Alaska). Feel free to do the same, and add to the list as you go. I'd love to hear about your finds at www.b-artise.com.

ALPHABETICAL, BY STATE

ALABAMA

Second Hand Rose
2015 Valleydale Rd., Suite 5
Birmingham 35244
205-987-7027
http://shrose.com

Zoe's Consignment in Forest Park
3900 Clairmont Ave. S
Birmingham 35222
205-595-9049
www.zoeshop.com

ALASKA

Plain Jane Consignment
113 W. Northern Lights Blvd.
Anchorage 99503
907-278-7227

Seconds to Go
360 Boniface Parkway
Anchorage 99504
907-333-6312

ARIZONA

A Second Look
Paradise Hills Shopping Center
10620 N. 32nd St.
Phoenix 85028-3202
602-992-1916
www.asecondlook.com

Desert Vintage & Costume
636 N. 4th Ave.
Tucson 85705
520-620-1570

How Sweet It Was
419 N. 4th Ave.
Tucson 85705
520-623-9854
www.howsweetitwas.com

The Old West Gallery
9615 Dateland
Tempe 85284
480-755-1901
www.theoldwestgallery.com

ARKANSAS

Cheap Thrills
120 South East Ave.
Fayetteville 72701
479-442-7735

Check My Closet Resale Shop
400 North Walton Blvd.
Bentonville 72712
479-273-3487

Designer Again
307 Garrison Ave.
Fort Smith 72901
479-782-8313

Encore Clothes
201 Public Square
Berryville 72616
870-423-4089

Jean's Good As New Consignment Shop
718 S. Church St.
Mountain Home 72653
870-424-5830
www.dd2k.com/parked/
jeansgoodasnew

CALIFORNIA

Brown Bear
289 Divisadero St.
San Francisco 94117
415-626-5779
www.brownbearsf.com

Brownies Vintage
2309 Encinal Ave., Ste. B
Alameda 94501
510-523-0112
+
2001 Milvia St.
Berkeley 94704
510-548-5955

Daisy Fairbanks / Ivy Company
930 41st Ave.
Santa Cruz 95062
831-477-9051
www.daisyfairbanks.com

Flashbacks
3849 5th Ave.
Hillcrest 92103
619-291-4200

Frock You Vintage Clothing
4121 Park Blvd.
San Diego 92103
619-220-0630
www.myspace.com/
frockyouvintage

Hubba Hubba
3220 W Magnolia Blvd.
Burbank 91505-2905
818-845-0636

Jabot's HollyVogue Boutique
3619 Union St.
Eureka 95503
707-445-8220
www.jabotsboutique.com

La Rosa Vintage
1711 Haight St.
San Francisco 94117-2807
415-668-3744

Park Place Vintage Clothing
1318 San Jose 95125
408-294-9893
www.parkplacevintage.com

Shareen Vintage
350 N. Ave. 21
Los Angeles 90031-1714
323-276-6226
www.shareenvintage.com

Squaresville
1800 N. Vermont Ave.
Los Angeles 90027-4213
323-669-8464

Wasteland
7428 Melrose Ave.
Los Angeles 90046-7515
323-653-3028
+
1660 Haight St.
San Francisco 94117-2816
415-863-3150

Vendima Vintage
4100 24th St.
San Francisco 94114
415-285-7174
www.vendimavintage.com

Wear It Again Sam
3823 5th Ave
San Diego 92103
619-299-0185
www.wearitagainsamvintage.com

COLORADO
Candy's Vintage Clothing & Costumes
4483 N. Broadway
Boulder 80304
303-442-6186
www.candysvintageclothing.com

First Class Trash
3330 S. Glen Ave.
Glenwood Springs 81601
970-945-0533

Repeat Boutique
2725 S. Colorado Blvd.
Denver 80222
303-757-0086
www.arepeatboutique.com

Second Impressions Limited
1635 W. Uintah St., Suite D
Colorado Springs 80904
719-227-6909

CONNECTICUT
Goatville Trading Co.
975 State St.
New Haven 06511
203-624-1140

Lorry Polizzi Vintage Clothing
2400 Foxon Rd
North Branford 06471
203-481-3730 2400

That Girl! Vintage Boutique
1089 S. Main St.
Cheshire 06410
203-271-0101
www.thatgirlvintageboutique.com

Twice-As-Nice
95 Lebanon Ave.
Colchester 06415
860-537-1213

The Willow Tree
4 Water St.
Chester 06412
860-526-4297

Yesterday's Threads Vintage Clothing
206 Meadows St.
Branford 06405
203-481-6452

DELAWARE
Clothes in the Past Lane
56 E. Main St.
Newark 19711
302-369-1960

Finders Keepers
901 Brandywine Blvd.
Wilmington 19809
302-762-7878

Sacks Thrift Avenue
800 Brandywine Blvd.
Wilmington 19809
302-762-1702
www.sacksthriftavenue.net

DISTRICT OF COLUMBIA
Annie Creamcheese
M Street
Georgetown
202-298-5555
www.anniecreamcheese.com

Clothes Encounters—Second Kind
202 7th St. SE
Washington DC 20003
202-546-4004

Meeps Vintage Fashionette
2104 18th St. NW
Washington, DC 20009
202-265-6546
www.meepsdc.com

Rainbow Store
823 H St. NE
Washington, DC 20002
202-547-2417

Remix Vintage
645 Pennsylvania Ave. SE
Washington, DC 20003
202-547.0211
www.remixvintage.com

FLORIDA

C. Madeleine's
13702 Biscayne Blvd.
North Miami 33181-1620
305-945-7770
shop.cmadeleines.com

Dechoes Resale Emporium
3207 Curry Ford Rd.
Orlando 32806
407-898-9791
dechoes.shoprw.com

Déjà Vu Vintage Clothing
1825 N. Orange Ave.
Orlando 32804
407-898-3609

Fly Boutique
650 Lincoln Rd.
Miami Beach 33139-2916
305-604-8508

Galerie
3733 S. Dixie Hwy.
West Palm Beach
561- 832-3611

Miami Twice
6562 SW 40th St.
Miami 33155-4830
305-666-0127
www.miami-twice.com

**Orlando Vintage Clothing
Company**
2117 W Fairbanks Ave.
Winter Park 32789-4507
407-599-7225

Sherry's Yesterdaze
5207 N. Florida Ave.
Tampa 33603-2139
813-231-2020
yesterdazevintage.com

Squaresville
508 Howard St.
Tampa Bay
813-259-9944
www.myspace.com/
squaresvilletampa

GEORGIA

Frock of Ages
1653 McLendon Ave. NE
Atlanta 30307
404-370-1006
www.frockofages.com

Junkman's Daughter
464 Moreland Ave. NE
Atlanta 30307
404-577-3188
www.myspace.com/
junkmansdaughteratlanta

The Lucky Exchange
212 Ponce De Leon Ave.
Atlanta 30308
404-817-7715
www.luckyexchange.com

Mix Sexy
4975 Jimmy Carter Blvd.
Norcross 30093
678-218-0754

Psycho Sisters
5964 Roswell Rd.
Atlanta 30326
404-255-5578
www.psychosistersshops.com

Stefan's Vintage Clothing
1160 Euclid Ave. NE
Atlanta 30307
404-688-4929
www.stefansvintage.com

HAWAII

Island Treasures Antique Mall
2301 Kuhio Avenue 2F
Waikiki Town Center
Waikiki 96815
808-922-8223
www.antique-central.com/hawaii.
html

Kilohana Clothing Co.
4-484 Kuhio Highway
Kapaa 96746
866-609-3703
www.kilohanaclothingco.com

IDAHO

Acquired Again Antiques
1304 Alturas St.
Boise 83702
208-338-5929

The Antique Hub
2244 Warm Springs Ave.
Boise 83712
208-336-4748

**Her Alibi Antiques and
Treasures**
211 S. 4th Ave.
Pocatello 83201
208-233-6797
www.heralibi.com

**Lux Fashion Lounge and
Vintage**
785 W. Idaho St. 83702
Boise
208-344-4589
+
225 N 5th St. 83702
Boise
208-433-8589
www.luxfashionlounge.com

**Picture Show Retro and
Vintage Clothing**
556 S. Vista Ave.
Boise 83705
208-344-7278

ILLINOIS

The Daisy Shop
67 E. Oak St., 6th Fl.
Chicago 60611
312-943-8880
daisyshop.com

Strange Cargo
3448 N. Clark St.
Chicago 60657-1610
773-327-8090
www.strangecargo.com

Wacky Cats
3012 N. Lincoln Ave.
Chicago 60657
773-929-6701
www.wackycats.com

INDIANA

Another Time Vintage Fashions
828 E. 64th St.
Indianapolis 46220
317-255-1277

Broad Ripple Vintage
824 E. 64th St.
Indianapolis 46220
317-255-4135

Red Rose Vintage Clothing
834 64th St
Indianapolis 46220
317-257-5016
www.rrnspace.com

Vintage Rose
E. Franklin St.
Nashville 47448
812-988-7283

IOWA
Barbara's Consignment Boutique
5601 Hickman Rd.
Des Moines 50310
515-274-1935

Dorothea's Closet
1733 Grand Ave.
Des Moines 50309
515-288-9982
www.dorotheasclosetvintage.com

Remember When Antiques
847 8th Ave.
Marion 52302
515-373-3039

Trash Can Annie
421 Brady St.
Davenport 52803
563-322-5893
www.trashcanannie.com

KANSAS
Avenue Thrift Store
927 Minnesota Ave.
Kansas City 66101
913-342-5363

Cristy's Closet Consignment Boutique
425 Delaware
Leavenworth 66048
913-651-5707

Harmonious Posh
611 W. Douglas
Wichita 67226
www.harmoniousposh.com

Orange Crate Gallery
714 SW Gage Blvd.
Topeka 66606
785-296-9207

Rockstar and Rogers Clothing and Costumes
715 N. 12th St.
Manhattan 66502
785-587-1819
www.myspace.com/
rockstarandrogers

Sugartown Traders
1024 Rhode Island St.
Lawrence 66044-3058
785-331-2791

Wild Man Vintage
939 Massachusetts St.
Lawrence 66044
785-856-0303

KENTUCKY
Ambiance Boutique Vintage and Collectables Gallery
964 Baxter Ave.
Louisville 40204
502-581-1200

Nitty Gritty Vintage Clothing and Wares
996 Barret Ave.
Louisville 40204
502-583-3377
www.nittygrittyvintage.com

2023 Antiques
2023 Frankfort Ave.
Louisville, 40206
502-899-9872

LOUISIANA
Funky Monkey
3127 Magazine St.
New Orleans 70115
504-899-5587

Miss Claudia's Vintage Clothing & Costumes
4204 Magazine St.
New Orleans 70115
504-897-6310

Trashy Diva
2048 Magazine St.
New Orleans 70130
504-299-8777
www.trashydiva.com

Turncoats Clothing Exchange
1926 Magazine St.
New Orleans 70130
504-299-9004

The Vintage Store at Star Hill
5181 US Hwy 61
St. Francisville 70775
225-635-6466
www.vintagevibes.com

MAINE
Another Chance Animal Rescue Thrift Shop
37 Market Street
North Berwick 03906
207-676-9330
www.acanimalrescue.org

Encore
521 Congress St.
Portland 04101
207-775-4275

Heart's Desire
191 Main St.
Saco 04072
207-282-6957

Material Objects
500 Congress St.
Portland 04101
207-774-1241

Outskirts Vintage Clothing
227 Broadway
Farmington 04938
207-778-4115

MARYLAND
Accessories of Old
4822 St. Elmo Ave.
Bethesda 20814
301-760-7228
www.accessoriesofold.com

Grammie's Attic
255 Market St. W, Suite 200
Gaithersburg 20878
www.grammies-attic.com

Killer Trash
602 S Broadway
Baltimore 21231
410-675-2449

Old Soul Vintage
20 Vine St.
Easton 21601
410-690-4878

Retropolitan
8006 Main St.
Ellicott City 21043
410-461-0701
www.retropolitan.net

Royal Vintage Clothing
2523 Gwynns Falls Pkwy.
Baltimore 21216
410-523-8664

MASSACHUSETTS
Cadia Vintage
148 Salem St.
Boston 02113
617-742-1203
http://cadiavintage.com

Closet Upstairs
223 Newbury St.
Boston 02116
317-267-5757

Garment District
200 Broadway
Cambridge 02139
617-876-5230
www.garment-district.com

History Consignment Boutique
1693 Massachusetts Ave.
Cambridge 02138
617-500-0868

Oona's
1210 Massachusetts Ave.
Cambridge 02138
617-491-2654

Sid Vintage
18 Crafts Ave.
Northampton 01060
413-582-9880
sid-vintage.com

Tangerine Boutique
110 Parker St.
Gardner
978-630-3488
tangerineboutique.com/tb_
shoppe.htm

MICHIGAN
Apple Anne's Vintage Clothing
29 E. Cross St.
Ypsilanti 48198
734-481-0555

Deco Doug
106 W. 4th St.
Royal Oak
248-547-3330

Lost and Found Vintage
510 S. Washington Ave.
Royal Oak 48067
248-548-6154
www.lostandfoundvintage.com/lfv

Mother Fletcher's
234 W. 9 Mile Rd.
Ferndale 48220
248-398-4816

Nicole's Revival
25525 West 7 Mile Rd.
Redford 48240
313-531-1234
www.nicolesrevival.com/home.
htm

Showtime Clothing
5708 Woodward Ave.
Detroit 48202
313-857-9280

MINNESOTA
Lula
1587 Selby Ave.
St Paul 55104
651-644-4110
www.stpaulretroloop.com

Rewind
2829 Johnson St. NE
Minneapolis 55418
612-88-9870
www.rewindminneapolis.com

Succotash
781 Raymond Ave.
St. Paul 55114
651-603-8787

Swank
1910 University Ave. W.
St. Paul 55104
651-646-5777
www.swankretro.com

Via's Vintage
2408 Hennepin Ave. S
Minneapolis 5405
612-74-3649
http://viasvintage.com

MISSISSIPPI
The Attic Vintage Clothing
116 3rd St. S
Columbus 39701
http://www.myspace.com/
atticville

**Decade Vintage Clothing &
Collectibles**
2927 North High St.
Columbus 43202
614-262-9046

L&L Odds & Ends Resale
614 Highway 51
Ridgeland 39157
601-853-9235

**The Mustard Seed Antique
Emporium**
1737 University Ave.
Oxford 38655
662-281-8004

Sugar Magnolia Antique Mall
1919 University Ave.
Oxford 38655
662-234-6330
sugarmagnoliaantiquemall.com

MISSOURI
Boomerang
1415 W. 39th St.
Kansas City 64111
816-531-6111

**Donna's Dress Shop Vintage
Clothing**
1415 W 39th St.
Kansas City 64111
816-561-6059
www.donnasdressshop.com

Dottie Mae's
7927 Wornall Rd.
Kansas City 64114
816-361-1505
www.dottiemaes.com

Re-Runs Vintage Apparel & Accessories of Distinction
4126 Pennsylvania Ave.
Kansas City 64111
816-561-4425
http://re-runs.com

MONTANA
Crazy Daisy Clothing Exchange
103 E. Main St.
Missoula 59802
406-549-1150

Gold Rush Adventures
211 W. Wallace St.
Sheridan 59749
406-843-5444

Montana Vintage Clothing
110 N. 29th St.
Billings 59101
406-248-7650
www.montanavintage.com

Mr. Higgins' Vintage Clothing and Costumes
612 S. Higgins
Missoula 59802
406-721-6446

Ranks Mercantile
416 W. Wallace St.
Sheridan 59749
406-843-5454

Rediscoveries Vintage Clothing
83 East Park St.
Butte 59701
406-723-2176

NEBRASKA
Circa Vintage Clothing
6058 Maple St.
Omaha 68104
402-553-5902

Rialto Extra
1725 O St.
Lincoln 68508
402-476-7680

Ruby Begonias
1321 P St.
Lincoln 68508
402-438-4438

Weird Wild Stuff Vintage Clothing Shop
4905 Leavenworth St.
Omaha 68106
402-551-7893
www.weird-wild-stuff.com

NEVADA
Annie Creamcheese
The Shoppes at the Palazzo
3327 Las Vegas Blvd.
Las Vegas 89109
702-452-9600
www.anniecreamcheese.com

The Attic
1018 S Main St.
Las Vegas 89101
702-388-2848
www.theatticlasvegas.com

Valentino's Zoot Suit Connection
906 S Sixth St.
Las Vegas 89101
702-383-9555
valentinoszootsuitconnection.com

NEW HAMPSHIRE
Off the Wall Clothing
31 Vaughan Mall
Portsmouth 03801
603-433-0023

R.H. Butler's Trading Company
102 First NH Turnpike (Rte 4)
Northwood 03261
nhantiquealley.com/
RSButlersTradingCompany.htm

Sak's Thrift Avenue
9 Main St.
Keene 03431
603-357-8070

Two Flights Down
171 Water St.
Exeter 03833
603-772-5988

Upscale Resale
278 State St.
Portsmouth 03801
603-431-2969

Wacky Jacky's
1020 Route 16
Ossipee 03864
603-539-1775

NEW JERSEY
Backward Glances
43 Broad St.
Red Bank 07701
732-842-9156

Gingerbread Consignment Shop
228 Godwin Ave.
Midland Park 07432
201-652-2814

Hala Vintage Clothing
326 5th St.
Jersey City 07302
201-653-8877
http://www.myspace.com/
halavintage

Marguerite's Consignment Shop
809 Main St.
Belmar 07719
732-280-6400

Mint
38 Bergen St.
Englewood 07631
201-894-8555
www.mintnj.com

My Friend's Closet
3003 State Highway No. 88
Point Pleasant Beach 08742
732-899-2626

Nostalgic Nonsense Vintage Clothing
903 Main St.
Belmar 07719
732-681-8810

Ragz to Riches
55 Kingsley
West Orange 07052
973-325-8255

Raid Gear
Mount Ephraim 08059
215-774-9874

Rave Girl
3710 US Highway 9
Freehold 07728
732-780-6849
+
Livingston Mall
Livingston 07039
973-533-0611

Repeat Performance
131 Kinderkamack Rd., Suite B
Park Ridge 07656
201-391-4086

Vintage Funk
219 Kings E.
Haddonfield 08033
856-354-4777

Ye Olde Thrift Shoppe
17 E. Front
Red Bank 07701
732-747-3013

NEW MEXICO

Act 2
839 Paseo De Peralta
Santa Fe 87501
505-983-8585

Claudy's Good As New
1425 N. Main St.
Clovis 88101
505-762-7984

Donna's Den
921 N. Main St.
Clovis 88101
505-763-7437

**Faerie Queen's Wild Things
Dress-Up Boutique**
316 Garfield St.
Santa Fe 87501
505-983-4908

Now & Again
229 Ranchitos Rd.
Taos 87571
505-737-5895

Regeneration Consignment
2740 Wyoming Blvd. NE
Albuquerque 87111
505-237-0022

2 Time Couture
600 Central Ave. SW
Albuquerque 87102
505-242-3600

NEW YORK

Fox & Fawn
112 Suffolk St.
New York 10002
212-375-1132
www.myspace.com/foxandfawn

Helen Uffner Vintage
345 W. 37th St.
New York 10018
212-253-2121
helenuffnervintageclothingllc.
visualnet.com

Screaming Mimi's
382 Lafayette St.
New York 10003
212-677-6464
www.screamingmimis.com

Tahir Boutique
75 Orchard St.
New York 10002
212-255-2121
www.tahirboutique.com

Night of Joy Vintage and Art
Rochester
585-520-7786
www.nightofjoyvintage.com/
about-us.htm

NORTH CAROLINA

Around Again Consignments
1830 E. Millbrook Rd.
Raleigh 27609
919-872-7283
http://aroundagain.com

Beggars & Choosers
38 Hillsboro St.
Pittsboro 27312
919-542-5884

Hip Replacements
72 N. Lexington Ave.
Asheville 28801
828-255-7573
hipreplacementsclothing.com

Hong Kong Vintage
2005 Central Ave.
Charlotte 28205
704-334-0538

**Time After Time Vintage
Thrift Shop**
414 W. Franklin St.
Chapel Hill 27516
919-942-2304

NORTH DAKOTA

109 Consign
109 Broadway N
Fargo 58102
701-280-0998

Exceptions
818 University Ave.
Grand Forks 58203
701-746-4626

Nearly New Shoppe
505 Riverwood Dr.
Bismarck 58504
701-222-1025

The What Not Shop
324 2nd St. W
Williston 58801
701-774-3000

Worn-A-Bit
211 S. Main Ave.
Rugby 58368
701-776-5089

OHIO

Captain Betty's
73 N. Sandusky St.
Delaware 43015
740-363-6739

Casablanca Vintage Clothing
3944 Spring Grove Ave.
Cincinnati 45223
513-541-6999

Déjà Vu
11 N. State St.
Westerville 43081
614-890-1130

Little Bit of Everything
216 E. Emmitt Ave.
Waverly 45690
740-941-0153

OKLAHOMA
Cheap Thrills Vintage
3018 E. 15th St.
Tulsa 74104
918-295-5868
www.cheapthrillsvintage.com

Deco to Disco Vintage
1508 E. 15th St.
Tulsa 74120
918-592-2070
www.decotodisco.com

Hopefully Yours
100 N. Broadway
Edmond 73034
405-341-6849

Elite Repeat Quality Resale
716 S. Main St.
Stillwater 74074
405-377-4462

Nearly New Buy Low Wear High
9218 N. Western Ave.
Oklahoma City 73114
405-848-4141

Next to New Shoppe
202 S. Main St.
Stillwater 74074
405-377-7209

Nut-N-New
614 Choctaw St.
Alva 73717
580-327-3394

The Re-Store
1234 NW 30th St
Oklahoma City 73118
405-525-7867

This Just In
808 E. Taft St.
Sapulpa 74066
918-248-4565

OREGON
Decades Vintage Company
328 SW Stark St.
Portland 97204
503-223-1177
www.decadesvintage.com

Hattie's Vintage
729 E. Burnside St., Ste 101
Portland 97214
503-238-1938

Magpie
520 SW Ninth Ave.
Portland 97205
503-220-0920

Red Light Clothing Exchange
3590 SE Hawthorne Blvd.
Portland 97214
503-963-8888

Xtabay
2515 SE Clinton St.
Portland 97202
http://xtabayvintage.blogspot.com

PENNSYLVANIA
Another Time Vintage Apparel
49 N. Main St.
Shrewsbury 17361
717-428-0297
anothertimevintageapparel.com

The Atomic Warehouse
1021 Market St.
Harrisburg 17101
717-236-1900
www.atomicwarehouse.com

Blendo
1002 Pine St.
Philadelphia 19107
215-351-9260

Crimes of Fashion
4628 Forbes Ave.
Pittsburgh 15213
412-682-7010

Hey Betty!
5892 Ellsworth Ave.
Pittsburgh 15232
412-363-0999

Vagabond
37 N. Third St.
Philadelphia 19106
267-671-0737
www.vagabondboutique.com

Yesterday's News
1405 E. Carson St.
Pittsburgh 15203
412-431-1712

Zap & Co.
315 N. Queen St.
Lancaster
717-397-7405
zapandco.com/home/index.html

RHODE ISLAND
2nd Appearance Fashions
1455 Mineral Spring Ave.
North Providence 02904
401-353-0099

Diva's Palace
299 Atwells Ave.
Providence 02903
401-831-0148

Exceptions Consignments
105 Franklin St.
Westerly 02891
401-596-1774

Foreign Affair Warehouse
219 Thayer St.
Providence 02906
401-274-1484

Into the Wardrobe
117 Brook St.
Providence 02906
401-831-7660

SOUTH CAROLINA
Annie's Attic
142 Arrow Road # B
Hilton Head Island 29928
843-686-6970

Ash and T's Furniture and Antiques Consignment Shop
900-C Bacon Bridge Rd.
Summerville 29483
843-851-6554
http://www.ashandts.com

Reruns Consignment Boutique
4555 Highway 17 By-Pass South
Myrtle Beach 29577
843-293-8388

Second Time Around
1300 E. Wade Hampton Blvd.
Greer 29651
864-877-3295

The Treasure Barn
1567 Ranger Drive (Hwy 6)
Cross 29436
843-753-4111

Turnabouts Chic Consignments
106 Jacob Smart Blvd.
Ridgeland,SC 29936
843-726-4340

SOUTH DAKOTA
Better Than Ever
3301 E. 26th St.
Sioux Falls 57103
605-336-3358

Sweet Repeat
830 N. Main St.
Spearfish 57783
605-642-3203

Twice Nice Clothing Consignment
318D W. 18th St.
Sioux Falls 57104
605-335-6538

Worth Repeating
103 East Kemp
Watertown 57201
605-882-4734

TENNESSEE
Hip Zipper Vintage Clothing
112 S. 11th St., Suite C
Nashville 37206
615-228-1942
www.hipzipper.com

Legacy Vintage Clothing
117 S. Central St.
Knoxville 37902
865-523-7335

Retro Pieces Vintage Clothing
211 Louise Ave.
Nashville 37203
615-329-3537.

Venus & Mars/Silvery Moon Vintage Clothing
2830 Bransford Ave.
Nashville 37204
615-269-8357
www.venusandmarsvintage.com

Vintage
411 Bridge St.
Franklin 37064
615-397-0555

TEXAS
Big Bertha's Bargain Basement
1050 S. Lamar Blvd.
Austin 78704
512-444-2382
bigberthasbargainbasement.com/frames.html

Blue Velvet
2100 Guadalupe St., Ste B
Austin 78705
512-472-9399
http://bluevelvetaustin.com/home

Counter Culture True Vintage
2707 Main St.
Dallas 75226
214-698-0117
+
Mockingbird Station
5331E. Mockingbird Ln.
Dallas 75206
214-414-1095
www.counterculturestore.com

Flipnotics
1603 Barton Springs Rd.
Austin 78704
512-322-9011
www.flipnotics.com

Gratitude Vintage Clothing
3714 Fairmount St.
Dallas 75219
214-522-2921

Pandemonium Limited
2726 N. Henderson Ave.
Dallas 75206
214-370-5677

Puttin' on the Ritz
6615 Snider Plaza
Dallas 75202
214-369-4015

Vintage Martini
1014 S. Broadway, Suite 100
Carrollton 75006
972-466-4400
www.vintagemartini.com

Way We Wore
2602 Waugh Dr.
Houston 77006
713-526-8910
www.thewaywewore.net

Zola's Everyday Vintage
2707 Main St.
Dallas 75226
214-698-0117
www.zolasvintage.com

UTAH
Decades Vintage Clothing
627 S. State St.
Salt Lake City 84111
801-537-1357

Grunts and Postures
779 E. 300 S.
Salt Lake City 84102
801-521-3202

Haroon's
461 Trolley Sq.
Salt Lake City 84102
801-322-5331

VERMONT
Battery Street Jeans Exchange
7 Marble Ave.
Burlington 05401
802-865-6223

Boomerang
12 Elliot St.
Brattleboro 05301
802-257-6911

Cream of the Crop Vintage Clothing
Stone House Antiques Center
Route 103
Chester 05143
802-875-6494

Listen Thrift Store
2 Maple Ave.
White River Junction 05001
802-295-9259

Twice Upon a Time
63 Main St.
Brattleboro 05301
802-254-2261
www.twicetime.com

VIRGINIA

Bygones Vintage Clothing
2916 W. Cary St
Richmond 23221
803-353-1919
www.bygonesvintage.com

Luxor Vintage Clothing
3001 W. Cary St.
Richmond 23221
804-359-6780

Vintage Swank
212 E. Main St.
Front Royal 22630
540-636-0069
www.vintageswank.com

Vogue Vintage
11414 Washington Plaza W.
Reston 20190
703-787-5700
www.voguetovintage.com

WASHINGTON

Last Waltz Boutique
1406 18th Ave.
Seattle 98122
206-328-5512
www.lastwaltzboutique.com

Le Frock
317 E. Pine St.
Seattle 98122
206-623-5339
www.lefrockonline.com

Pretty Parlor
119 Summit Ave. E
Seattle 98102
206-405-2883
www.prettyparlor.com

Stella Vintage
317 NW Gilman Blvd.
Issaquah 8027
425-92-2882

WEST VIRGINIA

It's New to You Consignment Shop
6464 Merritts Creek Rd.
Huntington 25702
304-736-3671

Retrodini
270 N. Washington St
Berkeley Springs 25411
304-258-7990
www.retrodini.com

Second Time Around
1003 3rd St.
New Martinsville 26155
304-447-1510

WISCONSIN

Attic Attire Consignment Boutique
201 Allen St
Clinton 53525
608-676-4015

Epoch Vintage Clothing
534 W. Washington Ave.
Madison 53703
608-255-2385

Joseph A Bank Clothiers
4301 W. Wisconsin Ave.
Grand Chute 54913
920-738-3934

My I.D.
101 W. Wisconsin Ave.
Pewaukee 53072
262-695-7565
my-industries.com/home.htm

Posh Threads
148 Fontana Blvd.
Fontana 53125
262-275-2707
www.poshthreads.net

Reflections of the Past
182 W. Main St.
Whitewater 53190
262-473-6050

Second Hand Quality
725 E. Wisconsin St.
Delavan 53115
262-728-0770

Tip Top Atomic Shop
2343 South Kinnickinnic Ave.
Milwaukee 53207
414-486-1951
www.tip-top-atomic.com

Torrence's House of Threads
275 W. Wisconsin Ave.
Milwaukee 53203
414-224-7848
+
4722 W. Fond Du Lac
Milwaukee 53216
414-445-0832

Twice as Nice
216 W. Wisconsin Ave.
Tomahawk 54487
715-453-8290
+
153 West Lincoln
Augusta 54722
715-286-4242
+
7646 N. Teutonia Ave.
Milwaukee 53209
414-355-4449

Vintage Vogue
115 5th Ave. S
La Crosse 54601
608-782-3722

WYOMING

Calamity Jane's Clothing Company
350 S. Washington St.
Afton 83110
307-885-9327
+
172 Short St.
Alpine 83128
307-654-9327

Ditto
15 W. 5th Ave.
Afton 83110
307-885-4050

Donna's Wear It Again
201 W. 17th St.
Cheyenne 82001
307-637-7005

The Hidden Treasure
222 S Main St
Lusk 82225
307-334-2324

2 Doors Down
1432 E. 2nd St.
Casper 82601
307-234-9791

GLOSSARY

A-LINE a silhouette fitted at the bust that flares our gradually to produce a shape similar to an "A"

APPLIQUÉ a separate piece of beaded or embroidered fabric applied to a garment

BABYDOLL a silhouette derived from women's sleepwear, the babydoll is shaped similiar to an A-line silhouette but with a empire waist (see below for definition)

BASTE loose, wide handsewn stitching used hold fabric in place and as a guide for machine stitching

BIB-STYLE a fabric insert placed just below the neck of a top or dress usually in a contrasting fabric

BODICE the part of a dress or tunic that covers the body from neckline to waist

BOLERO today's common shrug but was called bolero in the 80's usually with tapered arms and shoulder pads

CHENILLE a soft pile fabric similiar to velour, widely used for sweaters

CLOCHE close-fitting hat with a deep bell shaped crown

CONSIGNMENT STORE a store that takes in used clothing and pays the seller as they sell

EMBROIDERY FLOSS thread used for embroidery and other forms of needlework

EMPIRE WAIST a silhouette created by wearing a high-waisted dress, gathered near or just under the

bust with a long, loose skirt that skims the body

EPAULETTES a type of ornamental shoulder piece or decoration

FABRIC PEN a washable pen that allows you to mark a garment before sewing

FLOCKING applied pattern on velvet

GIMPS flat trimming made of silk or wool used to outline a design

HAND-SEW stitching with a needle and thread instead of a sewing machine

HOUNDSTOOTH woven or printed pattern of jagged checks

LAMÉ metallic fabric popular during the disco era

NATURAL WAIST by bending your body to the side (left or right) the crease it creates right above your hips is your natural waist

PRINCESS SEAMS long, shaped seams found on the front or back of a garment, used to achieve a tailored fit

RAW EDGE edge of garment before it is finished by zigzag stitch or serger

READY TO WEAR also known as prêt-à-porter, this is the fashion design term for clothing marketed in a finished condition, in standard clothing sizes

SATSUMA spectacular shade of orange derived from the Satsuma orange

SEAM ALLOWANCE adding extra length to your measurement to allow room to create a seam; prevents sewing too close to the edge of the fabric

SERGER a machine that finishes raw edges for a tailored look

SIZE INFLATION a ready-to-wear clothing phenomeon where nominal sizing has taken on larger dimensions over time

SPATS type of shoe accessory worn in the late 19th and early 20th Century, still worn today with band uniforms or on a haute couture fashion show

SWISS DOT A pattern of microdots with contrast stitiching which was a common vintage print

TAILOR'S CHALK a hard chalk used to make temporary markings on cloth

TOPSTITCH decorative stitching, usually near and parallel to a seam, sewn so as to be visible on the right side of a garment

TOQUE 16th-century style hat, usually velvet and brimless with a turned up brim

TUNIC a simple slip-on garment made with or without sleeves and usually knee-length or longer, originated from Ancient Greece

VANITY sizing similiar to size inflation by putting smaller numbers on bigger clothes

ZIGZAG STITCH a machine stitch that stitches a zigzag patern, used for decoration or to finish seams

INDEX

A

Arm warmers, 66, 119

B

Beads, 90
Bib-front tank top, 51, 104–105
Boot pants, 21, 81
Buttons, 90

C

Capelet, 36, 95
Cropped jacket, 40, 98–99

D

Denim bag, 52, 107–108
Dresses
 Halter dress, 76, 130–131
 Remix dress, 75, 126–127
 Strapless mini-dress, 71, 121–122
 Sweater mini-dress, 25, 85–86
 Sweater slipdress, 26, 87–88
 T-shirt dress, 47, 102
 Vintage combo dress, 65, 116–117

E

Evening gloves, 123

F

Fabiani, Alberto, 36
Fair-trade prices, 118
Flashdance (movie), 29

H

Halter dress, 76, 130–131
Hats, 128
High-waisted skirt, 60, 113
Hughes, John, 71

K

Knit cap with visor, 30

L

Leg warmers, 29, 89

M

Madonna, 35
Mini-poncho, 58, 112
Monroe, Marilyn, 84

N

National Button Society, 90

P

Pretty in Pink, 69

R

Remix dress, 75, 126–127
Reproduction patterns, 106
Resources, 134–139

S

Saturday Night Fever (movie), 39
Shorts, 55, 109–110
Sizing, 84
Strapless mini-dress, 71
Strapless top, 48, 103
Sweater corset, 35, 93–94
Sweater hoodie, 62, 115
Sweater mini-dress, 25, 85–86
Sweater slipdress, 26, 87–88

T

T-shirt blouse, 39, 51, 97
T-shirt dress, 47, 102
Tops
 Bib-front tank top, 51, 104–105
 Strapless top, 48, 103

V

Vintage combo dress, 65, 116–117
Vintage jumper, 72, 124–125

W

Wide belt, 43, 100
Winter vest, 22, 82–83